Off-Grid Oasis: DIY Projects for Sustainable Living

Empower Yourself with Creative Solutions for Off-Grid Independence

Noah Turner

Table of Contents

INTRODUCTION

"Off-Grid Oasis: DIY Projects for Sustainable Living" is an empowering e-book that provides a comprehensive guide for individuals seeking independence from conventional utilities and embracing a sustainable lifestyle. Authored by experts in off-grid living, this book presents a collection of creative and practical do-it-yourself (DIY) projects designed to help you achieve self-sufficiency and create your off-grid oasis.

In an era marked by environmental concerns, rising energy costs, and a growing desire for self-reliance, "Off-Grid Oasis" emerges as a beacon of inspiration. The e-book begins by laying the foundation for understanding the principles of off-grid living, exploring the benefits of sustainable practices, and offering insights into the challenges one might encounter on the journey toward independence. It then seamlessly transitions into a hands-on approach, providing readers with diverse DIY projects.

The projects featured in this e-book cover essential aspects of off-grid living, including energy generation, water management, food production, and shelter. From constructing solar panels and wind turbines to developing rainwater harvesting systems, each project is meticulously explained with step-by-step instructions and vivid illustrations and photographs. The emphasis on accessibility and affordability ensures these projects are feasible for individuals with varying technical expertise and financial resources.

"Off-Grid Oasis" is not just a technical manual; it's a guide that encourages readers to tap into their creativity and resourcefulness. It fosters a mindset of self-empowerment, enabling individuals to take control of their living conditions and reduce their ecological footprint. The e-book also addresses the importance of community building and collaboration, emphasizing that off-grid living is about personal independence and creating sustainable and resilient communities.

Whether you are a seasoned off-grid enthusiast or a newcomer intrigued by self-sufficiency, "Off-Grid Oasis" offers a wealth of knowledge and practical solutions. It is a roadmap for anyone looking to break free from the constraints of traditional living and embrace a more sustainable, environmentally conscious lifestyle. By delving into this e-book, your journey towards creating your off-grid oasis, where ingenuity meets sustainability and independence, becomes tangible.

CHAPTER I

Understanding Off-Grid Living

Exploring the principles of off-grid living

In a rapidly changing world dominated by modern conveniences and interconnected infrastructure, off-grid living challenges conventional norms and encourages self-sufficiency and sustainability. Off-grid life is living without utility grids for power, water, and other essentials. It is a conscious choice to liberate oneself from established systems and choose innovative, decentralized alternatives that allow individuals to manage their resources and environmental effects.

Off-grid living is about independence—becoming creators rather than consumers. Beyond rejecting prevalent luxuries, this mindset promotes resourcefulness, resilience, and a deep connection to nature. Living off the grid is a concept that promotes a sustainable relationship with the Earth.

Energy autonomy is crucial to off-grid life and sustainability. Leaving fossil fuels and their environmental implications behind, renewable energy sources are essential. Solar electricity, abundant and accessible, underpins off-grid energy. Solar panels and storage systems allow people to generate electricity, giving them more control over their power use and minimizing their dependence on networks.

Wind power is another critical off-grid energy source.

Wind power systems use turbines to convert wind energy into electricity. This decentralized energy-generating system provides stable and sustainable electricity in areas with predictable wind patterns. Wind power is a renewable energy source that contributes to a cleaner, more sustainable energy environment as people learn about it.

Micro-hydro power generation uses water's energy to demonstrate off-grid life. Individuals may use small hydroelectric systems to generate dependable electricity from streams and rivers. This method promotes sustainable use of local resources, environmental protection, and peace with nature.

Life requires water, another essential off-grid living premise. Rainwater harvesting is a novel way to manage water shortages decentralizedly. Rooftop rainwater collection and storage guarantees a sustainable water supply and decreases dependency on centralized water delivery systems. Well-digging and upkeep help people obtain groundwater for their requirements, boosting water self-reliance.

The ideals of off-grid living go beyond energy and water to include sustainable and regenerative lifestyle choices. These concepts are expressed in off-grid gardening, encouraging ecologically balanced food production. Off-grid farming requires organic, nutrient-rich soil, permaculture, and environmentally friendly activities. It emphasizes food self-sufficiency, land connection, and respect for nature's cycles.

Permaculture, a holistic design concept, emphasizes the human-environment connection to promote off-grid life. Designing sustainable landscapes that reflect nature's patterns and interactions promotes biodiversity, resilience, and environmental harmony. Off-grid living fosters stewardship of the land, sustainable ecosystems, and regenerative agriculture through permaculture.

In off-grid life, composting embodies recycling and trash reduction. A closed-loop system restores nutrients to the soil by turning organic kitchen and garden waste into nutrient-rich compost. People lessen their ecological impact by composting and regenerating soil, practicing sustainability and resource management.

Recycling and upcycling promote a circular economy, which supports off-grid life. Recycling produces new goods, reduces landfill waste, and conserves resources. Reusing materials creatively is upcycling, giving old goods new life. By adopting these habits, off-grid residents promote conscientious consumerism, waste reduction, and resource sustainability.

Off-grid living features, including eco-friendly materials, energy-efficient designs, and natural integration, are reflected in sustainable house construction. People develop sustainable houses using eco-friendly materials, energy-efficient technology, and designs. Minimalist tiny houses encourage people to reduce, value utility over excess, and value experiences over belongings.

Communication options for off-grid life emphasize digital self-sufficiency. Remote communication requires imaginative ways, including low-tech communication, off-grid networks, and technology that runs without centralized infrastructure. These communication methods help people stay connected and promote self-reliance and adaptation.

Off-grid living relies on DIY electronics to empower via creativity and ingenuity. Creating and sustaining off-grid electronics requires creating energy-efficient equipment, monitoring renewable energy sources, and finding connection options. DIY electronics allow people to customize technology and promote creativity and self-sufficiency.

Off-grid first aid implies readiness and self-sufficiency for health and well-being. First aid abilities for off-grid situations include learning fundamental medical procedures, making customized first-aid kits, and handling health problems in isolated areas. First aid concepts build resilience and self-reliance by preparing people for unexpected events.

Finally, learning about off-grid life inspires independence and sustainability. The path extends beyond energy, water, and food production. Off-grid living is a concept that challenges the current quo, inspires creativity, and creates a deep connection to the environment. By adopting off-grid living ideas, people rethink their connection with resources and start a more deliberate, self-sufficient, and peaceful life.

Environmental impact and benefits

The ever-growing human imprint on Earth has forced us to reconsider our society's decisions and their effects. In the context of worries about resource depletion, climate change, and environmental degradation, off-grid living concepts stand out as a revolutionary way to live that aims to reduce human effects on the environment while promoting harmonious cohabitation with the natural world. A strong understanding of how traditional living methods affect the environment and a dedication to adopting sustainable alternatives are at the core of this paradigm shift.

Living off the grid has several environmental advantages, chief among them being the decrease in carbon footprints brought about by energy use. Fossil fuel-based conventional energy generation is a significant source of greenhouse gas emissions. On the other hand, off-grid life encourages the use of renewable energy sources, including hydroelectric, solar, and wind power. Using the energy of the sun, wind, or moving water reduces the need for non-renewable resources, significantly reducing carbon emissions and lessening the adverse environmental effects of producing energy from fossil fuels.

The decentralized structure of off-grid energy systems also significantly reduces transmission and distribution losses, common in centralized grid systems. Traditional power grids sometimes require substantial infrastructure to transport electricity across large distances, which causes energy losses throughout the transmission process. By focusing on local energy production, off-grid living avoids these losses and promotes a more eco-friendly and effective energy use model.

Another critical environmental benefit of living off the grid is water saving. In off-grid systems, rainwater harvesting collects and stores rainwater for future use. This lessens dependency on centralized water delivery systems and offers a sustainable water source. Off-grid residents actively support the preservation of nearby ecosystems and eliminate energy-intensive water treatment procedures by reducing the demand for municipal water supplies.

Off-grid life encompasses more than just electricity and water; waste management is vital to environmental sustainability. In off-grid communities, recycling and upcycling are essential techniques that decrease trash transported to landfills and lessen the need for resource-intensive manufacturing processes. By adopting a circular economy philosophy, off-grid residents reduce the environmental effect of raw material extraction and processing by repurposing waste materials into new, valuable goods.

Building homes sustainably is a practical way to show that you are committed to reducing your influence on the environment. Off-grid homes are the pinnacle of a healthy coexistence between human habitation and the environment. They integrate structures with the natural terrain, use energy-efficient designs, and employ environmentally friendly building materials. Tiny homes, a minimalist form of living frequently connected to off- grid lives, encourage smaller living areas that take less resources to build and maintain, which helps to save the environment further.

Off-grid lifestyle concepts place a strong emphasis on sustainable and regenerative agricultural methods. Permaculture and off-grid gardening emphasized ecological harmony, biodiversity, and organic farming. These methods improve soil quality and protect regional ecosystems by reducing the need for artificial fertilizers and pesticides. Off-grid farmers who follow these guidelines provide a reliable food source and actively contribute to sustainable agriculture, reducing the adverse environmental effects of industrial agricultural methods.

One further advantage of off-grid living for the environment is the decreased need for traditional transportation methods. Off-grid residents reduce the need for lengthy trips to obtain resources by promoting localized and sustainable habits. This lowers transportation-related carbon emissions and strengthens linkages to nearby communities and ecosystems. The focus on self-sufficiency also includes local manufacturing of products and services, which helps to lessen the environmental impact of long-distance commerce and transportation.

Furthermore, the ideas of off-grid life promote a more tremendous respect and knowledge of nature. Living in peace with nature means having a keen understanding of seasonal variations, local ecosystems, and the effects of human activity on the environment. Off-grid living encourages a sense of stewardship and responsibility via ecological consciousness, which motivates people to take an active role in biodiversity preservation, habitat restoration, and conservation.

Off-grid living has obvious environmental benefits, but it's also essential to recognize the drawbacks and difficulties that come with it. Off-grid systems must be carefully planned, maintained, and adjusted to the local environment. Because renewable energy sources, like wind and sunshine, are intermittent, reliable energy storage is necessary to provide a steady electricity supply. Off-grid living may also offer early financial difficulties because sustainable building, water management infrastructure, and renewable energy systems have more significant upfront expenditures than traditional options.

In summary, the advantages and effects of off-grid living on the ecosystem highlight a fundamental change in how people relate to the environment. Off-grid living emphasizes ecological harmony, self-sufficiency, and sustainability, allowing off-grid residents to participate actively in international efforts to mitigate environmental concerns. Together, the ideas of cutting back on energy use, preserving water, cutting waste, and adopting regenerative agricultural techniques provide a comprehensive strategy that minimizes the ecological impact and strengthens ties to the natural world. Off-grid living is a shining example of how a peaceful and sustainable coexistence with nature is a romantic concept and an honest and transforming way of life in an era of increased environmental consciousness.

Realities and challenges of living off-grid

Many people looking for an alternative to the typical metropolitan way of life have been captured by the appeal of off-grid living because it promises self-sufficiency, sustainability, and a greater connection to nature.

Nevertheless, the varied realities and problems that those who start on this trip must face are hidden behind the idealized pictures of off-grid cottages, renewable energy systems, and flourishing gardens. One must have a fundamental awareness of the realities involved, a dedication to resilience, and a desire to traverse the difficulties inherent in crafting an independent and sustainable living to decide to live off-grid. This lifestyle choice may ultimately alter one's life.

Off-grid living necessitates a significant mental and behavioral adjustment, one of the most essential requirements for this way of life. It is no longer possible to take for granted the advantages that come with living in a modern urban environment, such as electric power that is easily accessible, readily available water, and communication networks. Those who live off the grid must adopt a more deliberate and conscientious approach to their day-to-day activities. They must acknowledge that resources, including water, energy, and resources, are limited and must be managed cautiously. Not only does this shift in mentality include adjusting to alternative technology, but it also involves cultivating tremendous respect for the conservation of resources and a heightened awareness of the influence of individual activities on the environment.

Energy autonomy is a fundamental component of off-grid life, yet the practical realities of utilizing renewable energy sources provide several problems and benefits. Solar power, which is frequently hailed as a critical off-grid energy source, is contingent on the availability of sunshine, making it intermittent and vulnerable to weather circumstances. In a similar vein, wind power systems are dependent on the presence of persistent wind patterns. In contrast, the generation of micro-hydro power depends on running water availability. To guarantee a constant supply of electricity, it is necessary to have a reliable energy storage system, often in the form of batteries. This is because the renewable sources themselves are inherently variable. To successfully live off the grid, individuals must acquire the skills to optimize energy consumption, monitor systems, and organize activities around available resources. Understanding and controlling these energy dynamics becomes an essential component of off-grid life.

In off-grid living, where access to water is frequently decentralized and dependent on natural sources, water, an essential resource for continued existence, takes on a new significance. Collecting and storing rainwater for use in home settings can be referred to as rainwater harvesting, and it is becoming increasingly widespread. Although this provides an environmentally favorable alternative to conventional water supplies, it also necessitates careful planning, appropriate filtering methods, and establishing storage facilities. There is also the possibility of digging wells and maintaining them, providing access to groundwater. On the other hand, geological considerations and the careful management of these water sources are the two most essential elements determining the quality and sustainability of healthy water. People who live off the grid must overcome the issues of securing a stable and drinkable water supply while limiting the impact on the environment.

It is essential to the lifestyle that you build a home that is both environmentally friendly and compatible with living off the grid. Choosing eco-friendly materials, optimizing designs for energy efficiency, and integrating the structure in a harmonious way with the natural surroundings are just a few of the components involved in sustainable house building. The practical realities require navigating local building rules, finding sufficient property, and frequently confronting higher initial construction expenses. This aligns with the ideas of environmental responsibility; nevertheless, the realities involve these additional challenges. Tiny houses, a popular off-grid dwelling solution, provide a minimalist alternative; nonetheless, the design and construction of these homes require careful thought of how space is utilized, how utility is achieved, and how effectively rules are adhered to.

The realities of gardening without access to a grid shed light on the many facets of growing one's food stock. The concepts of organic farming, permaculture practices, and composting all contribute to sustainability, yet off-grid gardeners face challenges that include soil quality, climate differences, and the control of pests. A continuous learning process involves developing the skills and knowledge essential for practical gardening, and the yield may only sometimes be sufficient to fulfill the family's immediate requirements. Therefore, to achieve self-sufficiency in food production, it is necessary to plan diligently, adjust to the conditions of the local environment, and commit to accepting the unpredictability of nature.

Communities not connected to the grid frequently push for the implementation of permaculture, a holistic design approach that blends human activities with natural ecosystems. Even though its principles are congruent with sustainable living, putting permaculture into practice calls for an in-depth comprehension of ecological patterns, biodiversity, and behaviors that promote regeneration. Continuous observation, experimentation, and adaptation are required elements in designing and sustaining a landscape influenced by permaculture. Recognizing that permaculture is a dynamic and developing approach to sustainable land use, people who live off the grid must manage the intricacies of balancing aesthetic concerns, food production, and the ecosystem's health.

Off-grid living poses a unique challenge regarding trash management, highlighting the significance of recycling, upcycling, and reducing the overall amount of garbage produced. Even though these principles align with environmental conservation, the practicalities include developing inventive ways to reuse materials, building composting systems, and disposing of waste that cannot be recycled responsibly. People who live off the grid have to deal with a restricted garbage disposal infrastructure, which requires them to develop creative solutions to recycle items and reduce their environmental impact.

Regarding off-grid life, communication in rural areas presents a distinct set of obstacles that must be overcome simultaneously. Creative solutions, such as satellite internet, radio communication, and other off-grid connection possibilities, are required to establish communication networks that are dependable and effective. Navigating the trade-offs between connectivity, energy consumption, and cost becomes an ongoing activity. It requires individuals to strike a balance between the demand for communication and the constraints of the technologies that are now accessible.

One further essential component of off-grid life is the use of do-it-yourself electronics, which allow folks to construct and maintain their technical systems. Even though this is in line with the values of self-sufficiency and innovation, it requires the acquisition of technical skills, the ability to troubleshoot problems, and the ability to keep up with the latest breakthroughs in renewable energy technology. A dedication to continuous learning, the ability to adapt to ever-evolving technology, and the ability to solve the specific obstacles that are presented by off-grid situations are all realities of do-it-yourself electronics creation.

The provision of off-grid first aid highlights the significance of health and safety in settings where access to emergency services may be restricted. Several vital parts of readiness include acquiring first aid skills, creating complete first aid supplies, and knowing the health concerns of living off the grid. Developing medical expertise, maintaining a current understanding of first aid procedures, and being prepared to deal with various health issues in distant regions are all realities that must be faced.

One of the realities of living off the grid is that it comes with many problems and significant perks. Engaging in this way of life fosters a profound sense of independence, resiliency, and connectedness to the natural world. People who live off the grid frequently express a greater understanding of contentment with a less complicated and purposeful lifestyle in which the natural cycles of the seasons and the earth influence their daily activities. In forming a community of persons dedicated to environmental stewardship and self-sufficiency, the problems transform into possibilities for personal development, professional advancement, and adaptability.

The realities and difficulties of living off the grid reflect a varied path towards self-sufficiency and sustainability. Even though it necessitates a change in mentality, continuous education, and the capacity to adjust to the area's circumstances, the lifestyle provides a one-of-a-kind and life-altering way of living. A comprehensive strategy is necessary to successfully navigate the challenges of energy autonomy, water management, sustainable building, gardening, waste reduction, and communication. Individuals are given the ability to form a meaningful and deliberate relationship with the environment through the process of off-grid living, which is not a solution that is universally applicable but rather a dynamic and individualized journey. The realities and difficulties of living off the grid are becoming more critical components of a way of life that strives to promote resiliency, environmental responsibility, and a strong feeling of autonomy. This is because more individuals are exploring living off the grid.

CHAPTER II

The Off-Grid Lifestyle

Advantages and Challenges

The decision to live off the grid is a transformative option that comes with a variety of distinct advantages as well as obstacles. Ultimately, the quest for autonomy, self-sufficiency, and a more harmonious relationship with the environment is at the heart of the fascination associated with living off the grid. However, this lifestyle choice has its complexity, and it is necessary to carefully consider the benefits that attract individuals to this road and the difficulties that may occur in the pursuit of independence.

Living off the grid allows one to pursue energy independence, which is one of the critical advantages of this lifestyle choice. Individuals residing in traditional residences are vulnerable to power outages and the unpredictability of external energy sources because these homes primarily depend on centralized power infrastructures. On the other hand, individuals who are interested in off-grid living generate power through renewable resources such as solar panels, wind turbines, and micro-hydro systems. In addition to ensuring a steady and dependable supply of energy, this also helps lessen the impact on the environment, which contributes to a more environmentally responsible way of life. Individuals can use power and contribute to a more ecologically friendly future when they have the potential to create their own energy. This fosters a sense of empowerment.

A profound connection to nature and a simplified way of life are two benefits of living off the grid, in addition to the independence from fossil fuels. Individuals are encouraged to engage more intimately with their surroundings when they can eliminate their dependence on modern comforts. The lifestyle emphasizes a greater understanding and respect of natural cycles, whether through cultivating an off-grid garden, relying on rainwater gathering, or the construction of an environmentally appropriate shelter. Off-grid residents develop a greater awareness of the influence of their decisions on the ecosystems in their immediate vicinity as a result of this connection, which in turn helps to cultivate a feeling of environmental stewardship.

Another appealing advantage of living off the grid is engaging in sustainable agriculture. Cultivating one's own food becomes an essential discipline, which encourages self-sufficiency and lessens dependency on food sources obtained from outside sources. Off-grid gardening incorporates strategic planning, companion planting, and permaculture concepts to provide a comprehensive approach to food production. The advantages are not limited to merely providing sustenance; they also include the benefits to one's health, the reduction of expenses, and a deeper connection to the food humans consume. With the cultivation of a wide variety of crops and the implementation of regenerative methods, off-grid living contributes to the development of a food system that is both healthier and more robust.

In the context of off-grid living, waste management takes on a new meaning, transforming it into an opportunity for resourcefulness and innovation. Through composting, organic waste can be converted into beneficial soil amendments, completing the nutrient cycle. Composting is an essential technique. Individuals are encouraged to repurpose resources and limit the amount of garbage they produce through do-it-yourself recycling and upcycling projects, which further lessen the overall impact of consumerism on the environment. The benefits of these activities extend beyond the local off-grid context and contribute to a more comprehensive philosophy of preserving the environment and responsible utilization of resources.

The ability to design homes that are both sustainable and kind to the environment is one of the primary benefits of living off the grid. Typical houses are typically constructed using resource-intensive materials and designs that are energy-intensive. On the other hand, off-grid homes emphasize environmentally friendly materials and designs that minimize energy consumption and

frequently
adhere to the minimalist philosophy. This desire to live compactly and efficiently is exemplified by the popularity of tiny houses among those interested in living off the grid. In the realm of sustainable home construction, do-it-yourself projects allow individuals to design homes that not only fulfill their fundamental requirements but also reduce their negative impact on the environment.

The benefits of off-grid technologies extend far beyond the conveniences of living in the modern world. Even though the way of life promotes a reduction in reliance on technology, it also calls for the development of realistic solutions for connectivity in geographically isolated locations. Off-grid communication devices, satellite internet, and do-it-yourself electronics projects are all viable options to satisfy the fundamental requirement for communication and connectivity. The acquisition of skills in off-grid technology allows individuals to troubleshoot and maintain electronic devices, fostering self-reliance in a world that is becoming increasingly linked.

Off-grid living allows individuals to consciously equip themselves to manage unforeseen problems, which is a significant advantage from an emergency preparedness standpoint. An essential component of living an off-grid lifestyle is building do-it-yourself first aid kits, acquiring fundamental medical training, and formulating evacuation plans. This proactive strategy guarantees that people who live off the grid are well-prepared to deal with unexpected crises and catastrophes, contributing to a heightened sense of resilience and self-sufficiency among these individuals.

Living off the grid has several problems, even though it offers many benefits. One of the most significant challenges is the initial investment of money and labor necessary to set up off-grid systems. The initial cost commitment may be high when investing in sustainable technologies such as solar panels, wind turbines, and similar technologies; however, the long-term savings and environmental advantages typically outweigh the original financial commitment. Additionally, living off the grid requires a lot of research and learning on the part of individuals, as they need to gain new skills in areas such as sustainable agriculture, energy systems, and do-it-yourself construction practices.

One further significant obstacle is the requirement for managing resources in a disciplined manner. Because they are responsible for creating and maintaining their supply, those who live off the grid need to become proficient in conserving energy, water, and other resources. Because of this, it is necessary to make a concerted effort to reduce waste, make optimal use of resources, and adopt a mindful approach to consumption. Individuals accustomed to the ease of contemporary amenities may find it challenging to transition to live off the grid because it involves a change in thinking and behaviors.

In addition, the off-grid lifestyle may provide difficulties in terms of social and cultural aspects. When you live in a location that is removed from traditional towns and urban hubs, you may experience feelings of isolation. It may be necessary for those who live off the grid to adjust to a more solitary way of life, mainly if the region they choose is remote. It is vital to establish an off-grid and supportive community to facilitate the exchange of information, resources, and experiences, thereby lessening the possible difficulties associated with being isolated.

Living off the grid presents a complex picture of a lifestyle that stresses sustainability, self-sufficiency, and a greater connection to nature. In conclusion, the advantages and challenges of off-grid living create a compelling picture of this lifestyle. The revolutionary potential of off-grid life is highlighted by its benefits, which include energy independence and sustainable agriculture, as well as an increased sense of resilience and preparation. On the other hand, the difficulties, which have the initial expenses, the requirement for resource discipline, and the possibility of social isolation, call for careful thinking as well as a dedication to the acquisition of knowledge and adaptation. In the end, for individuals who choose to live an off-grid existence, the trip is not only about disconnecting from the grid; it is an all-encompassing investigation into a way of living that is more purposeful, sustainable, and satisfying.

Embracing a Sustainable Mindset

In a society struggling to deal with environmental issues and a climate disaster that is on the horizon, the encouragement to adopt a sustainable attitude is louder than ever. Individuals are encouraged to see the connectivity between human activities and the world's health when they embrace sustainability, which is not only a fad but a fundamental shift in viewpoint. This article investigates the essence of adopting a sustainable mentality, focusing on the basic concepts, the influence of individual decisions, and the transformational potential of a collective commitment to environmental stewardship.

The fundamental foundation of a sustainable mentality is the concept that human actions should try to fulfill present needs without compromising the ability of future generations to meet their own needs. This understanding is the foundation of a sustainable mindset. It is a realization of the fact that the resources of the Earth are limited in quantity, as well as an understanding that responsible stewardship is necessary for the long-term health of the planet. The concept of sustainability encompasses not just the environmental aspect but also the economic, social, and cultural aspects. As a comprehensive approach, it tries to balance these many aspects, building resilience and assuring the flourishing of ecosystems and communities.

The development of a sustainable mentality mostly depends on individuals' actions and decisions. All of the decisions that we make in our day-to-day lives, from the kinds of goods that we buy to the modes of transportation that we use, contribute to our overall influence on the environment. Adopting sustainable practices requires making conscious decisions, such as selecting things that can be reused rather than those that are disposable, limiting the amount of energy consumed, and assisting ecologically responsible enterprises. The notion of a sustainable mentality extends beyond personal habits; it impacts more extensive lifestyle choices, career routes, and even how individuals interact with the communities in which they live.

Knowing that the choices that consumers make have a substantial impact is one of the fundamental components of adopting a sustainable lifestyle. More often than not, modern consumer society is defined by a culture of excessive consumption and the use of disposable products. This worldview is challenged by adopting a sustainable attitude, which encourages consumption that is conducted with consideration. Considering the environmental and social repercussions of products, assisting businesses that exhibit ethical business practices, and prioritizing quality over quantity are all components of this approach. Individuals may help the transition toward a more sustainable economy that emphasizes durability, repairability, and responsible manufacturing processes by selecting items with a low environmental impact.

The built environment, which includes residential areas, places of employment, and infrastructure, is an essential arena in which sustainable decisions have the potential to have a significant influence. In addition to lowering the environmental footprint, the design and construction of buildings that incorporate energy efficiency, renewable energy sources, and sustainable materials create healthier and more robust living environments and reduce this footprint. Building communities at peace with the environment, fostering biodiversity, and limiting the effects of urban heat islands are all outcomes that may be achieved via adopting sustainable design and urban planning concepts. Furthermore, the lifespan and flexibility of the built environment are both contributed to by the retrofitting of existing structures to satisfy sustainability criteria.

Taking into account the usage of energy is an essential component of the equation for sustainability. To lessen our dependency on limited fossil fuels and reduce greenhouse gas emissions, it is necessary to embrace renewable energy sources such as solar, wind, and hydropower. Contributing to the fight against climate change on a global scale are individuals, communities, and governments going through the process of converting to renewable energy. Additionally, the conservation of energy through the implementation of better efficiency measures plays a complementary complement of energy-efficient appliances, the reduction of trash, and the adoption of sustainable mobility choices all contribute collectively to a more sustainable energy picture.

The transportation sector, a substantial contributor to carbon emissions, presents an enticing opportunity to implement environmentally responsible practices. We are committed to decreasing mobility's negative impact on the environment, and this dedication is shown in the transition toward electric automobiles, public transportation, cycling, and walking. When it comes to transportation, adopting a sustainable mindset goes beyond making choices on an individual level; it also involves advocating for and supporting the development of public transportation systems that are comprehensive and accessible, infrastructure for cycling and walking, and policies that incentivize sustainable transportation alternatives.

Agriculture, which is crucial to the development of human civilization, is yet another field in which adopting a sustainable attitude is of the utmost significance. Conventional agricultural techniques frequently entail the significant use of pesticides, herbicides, and synthetic fertilizers, which contribute to soil deterioration, water contamination, and biodiversity loss. Adopting regenerative agricultural methods that emphasize soil health, biodiversity, and water conservation is involved in adopting sustainable agriculture. Permaculture and organic farming are two examples of agroecological practices that align with sustainability ideals. These practices encourage a resilient and harmonious ecosystem between agriculture and the environment. When it comes to water management, adopting a sustainable attitude should also be considered. One of the most critical challenges facing the world today is water shortage, which is made worse by climate change and wasteful water usage. Conservation, responsible management of water resources, and effective use of water are the three components that comprise sustainable water practices. Individuals can do so by minimizing the amount of water wasted in their houses, promoting water-efficient technology, and lobbying for legislation that prioritizes environmentally responsible water management methodologies.

Education is one of the most critical factors in developing a sustainable mentality because it equips individuals with the information and awareness that facilitates the making of informed decisions. Incorporating sustainability into the school curriculum may foster a better understanding of environmental challenges, the interconnection of ecosystems, and the ramifications of human actions on the world. It promotes a feeling of environmental responsibility by providing individuals with the resources necessary to critically analyze information, criticize activities that are not sustainable, and advocate for transformational solutions.

Businesses, which are powerful actors in the economy of the entire world, significantly influence the concept of sustainability. Regarding business, adopting a sustainable mentality requires incorporating environmental, social, and governance (ESG) elements into the decision-making process. The management of ethical supply chains, reducing carbon footprints, and prioritizing social responsibility are all fundamental components of sustainable business operations. Companies that implement sustainable practices contribute to the preservation of the environment and position themselves as leaders in a shifting economic landscape where customers increasingly value ethical and sustainable business models.

How the international community has responded to the issue of climate change is illustrative of the transformational potential that may be achieved by adopting a sustainable attitude on some level. International accords and efforts, such as the Paris Agreement, highlight the critical need for global collaboration to combat climate change and advance sustainable practices. Because of the linked nature of environmental problems, it is necessary to work together to find solutions, which requires overcoming country boundaries and cultural divides. To adopt a sustainable mentality on a global scale, it is essential to acknowledge that we all share responsibility for the world's well-being and collaborate to provide new solutions and bring about systemic change.

In conclusion, adopting a sustainable mentality is a process of transformation that starts with a person's choices and extends to include communities, industries, and society as a whole. A fundamental shift in viewpoint is required, one that places value on the delicate balance between the actions of humans and the well-being of the world we live in. By implementing sustainable practices in areas such as consumption, architecture, energy, transportation, agriculture, water management, education, and business, individuals can contribute to a more harmonious relationship with the environment. The potential of a sustainable mentality to modify behaviors, impact societal norms, and inspire a collective commitment to environmental stewardship is the source of this mindset's transformational power. In navigating the problems that the 21st century presents to humanity, adopting sustainable practices becomes a choice and a vital necessity for the well-being of both the current generation and the generations to come.

CHAPTER III

Energy Independence

Solar Power Essentials

There has been increased attention to solar power as the globe struggles to meet the dual energy consumption problems and maintain environmental sustainability. The utilization of solar energy, derived from the sun's plentiful and sustainable rays, is an essential component in transitioning towards environmentally friendly and sustainable energy solutions. In this article, we go into the fundamentals of solar power, examining its fundamental concepts, technical breakthroughs, applications across various industries, and the revolutionary role it plays in determining the future of energy landscapes worldwide.

The technique of photovoltaics (PV), a technology that creates energy by directly converting sunlight into electricity, is the fundamental component of solar power. In the form of photons, the sun, a massive nuclear fusion reactor, is responsible for the emission of enormous quantities of energy. Through the process known as the photovoltaic effect, these photons can create an electric current when they come into contact with the surface of solar cells that are composed of semiconductor materials such as silicon. Solar photovoltaic systems are built on the foundation of this frictionless conversion of sunlight into electrical power. Throughout the years, solar panels have seen substantial breakthroughs in their effectiveness in capturing sunlight. Continual research and development activities have spearheaded these advancements.

Because of its inherent sustainability and kindness to the environment, solar power is considered one of the most advantageous forms of energy. Solar energy, in contrast to traditional energy sources such as fossil fuels, is not only abundant but also cannot be depleted, and it does not release damaging greenhouse gases while producing electricity. Through a reduction in reliance on fossil fuels and a reduction in the carbon footprint connected with the generation of electricity, the utilization of solar power contributes to the mitigation of climate change. The environmental advantages are not limited to the reduction of emissions; they also include a decrease in the demand for water resources, which is an essential factor to consider in areas struggling with water shortages.

A wide range of industries may benefit from the diversity of solar power applications, which provide a varied solution to the problem of energy requirements. In the residential sector, rooftop solar systems allow homeowners to produce their own electricity, enabling them to reduce their dependency on the grid and thus reduce their monthly utility costs. Governments and corporations are boosting their investments in large-scale solar farms, which can harness massive swaths of land to provide renewable energy for whole towns. Solar power has the potential to be of great benefit to off-grid and isolated locations since it may provide access to energy in areas where the establishment of regular power infrastructure would be economically prohibitive.

The advancements that have been made in solar technology have made novel applications that go beyond the scope of conventional solar panels possible. Using building-integrated photovoltaics, also known as BIPV, solar cells may be smoothly incorporated into building materials, transforming buildings into energy-generating assets. Solar windows, also known as transparent solar cells, can convert sunlight into electricity while preserving transparency. This opens the possibility of energy- efficient buildings with increased natural illumination. The creation of solar-powered vehicles, which can include automobiles and even aircraft, is a significant step toward environmentally responsible transportation.

Storage solutions are paramount when managing the intermittent nature of solar power generation. The ability to harvest and store extra energy during abundant sunshine for later usage in times of limited sunlight is made possible by energy storage equipment such as batteries. This technology not only makes it possible to have a more dependable and continuous supply of electricity, but it also helps to maintain the stability of the grid, reducing the requirement for backup power plants powered by fossil fuels.

The use of solar power has substantial economic repercussions, including providing employment opportunities, accelerating technical innovation, and the promotion of energy independence. Due to the exponential expansion that the solar sector has seen, career possibilities are now available in various fields, including research and development, production, installation, and maintenance. Solar power is becoming increasingly competitive with traditional energy sources as solar technology costs decrease. This, in turn, makes solar power an economically feasible choice for both developed and developing nations.

In the transition to a global energy system, solar power is essential in accomplishing sustainability objectives and reducing reliance on limited fossil fuel supplies. Solar installations of varying scales, which promote the decentralization of energy production, contribute to energy security by lowering susceptibility to centralized power generation systems. This is accomplished through the decentralization of energy production. Countries that make investments in solar infrastructure position themselves as leaders in the worldwide move towards renewable energy. These countries not only get environmental benefits but also gain geopolitical advantages.

Even though solar power has many benefits, several obstacles still need to be overcome before it can become widely used. There are issues associated with the creation of constant energy due to the intermittent nature of sunlight and the dependency on weather conditions. Grid integration and storage solutions are two options that can help solve some of these difficulties; nevertheless, developments in energy storage technologies are necessary to overcome limits associated with energy availability. Furthermore, there are issues regarding the environmental effect of the manufacture and disposal of solar panels, which highlights the necessity of implementing sustainable practices across the whole lifespan of solar technology.

The research and development efforts to improve solar power are centered on improving its efficiency, durability, and sustainability as it continues to gain significance. Thin-film solar cells, organic solar cells, and perovskite solar cells are all examples of ongoing research being conducted to enhance the efficiency of solar technology while simultaneously lowering its negative impact on the environment. To overcome the problems that are now present and realize the full potential of solar power, technological advancements, in conjunction with supportive policies and investments, play a critical level of importance.

Through the incorporation of solar power into innovative grid systems and the introduction of digital technology, the influence that solar power has on energy systems has been further amplified. Intelligent grids make it possible for energy producers and consumers to communicate effectively, resulting in real-time optimization of energy distribution and consumption. As a result of this integration, grid resilience is improved, energy waste is reduced, and the dynamic character of solar power output is accommodated.

The move towards renewable energy sources is an absolute necessity to address climate change, and global efforts and legislative frameworks, such as the Paris Agreement, highlight the importance of this transition. Financial incentives, government subsidies, and regulatory frameworks are being implemented by governments worldwide to stimulate the use of solar power. The global community has agreed on the significance of sustainable energy practices, as seen by the commitment to renewable energy objectives and the subsequent elimination of subsidies for fossil fuels.

Both people and local communities are given the ability to actively engage in the transition to solar power through the implementation of community-driven initiatives and decentralized energy projects. There is a democratization of access to renewable energy through the implementation of community solar projects. These projects include stakeholders cooperatively investing in and benefiting from a shared solar system. Not only can these efforts improve energy resilience at the community level, but they also develop a sense of ownership and responsibility for environmentally responsible actions.

Apart from its direct function as a source of energy, solar power possesses the potential to bring about significant transformations. It acts as a catalyst for redesigning the larger energy environment, questioning the paradigms that are now in place, and driving a paradigm shift toward sustainability. The conventional dynamics of power generation and consumption are being reshaped due to the democratization of energy production and developments in storage and grid technology.

Education is a significant factor in cultivating a more comprehensive grasp of the fundamentals of solar power. People can make educated decisions regarding their energy use and advocate for sustainable practices when they participate in programs that promote solar literacy. These programs may be found in schools as well as community outreach initiatives. The educational efforts contribute to developing a society that values the transition to renewable energy and actively participates in it. This is accomplished by demystifying the science that lies behind solar power and stressing the real benefits that it offers.

Solar power is essential in the broader effort to find environmentally friendly and sustainable energy solutions worldwide. Solar power is positioned to become a revolutionary force in the energy landscape due to its ability to harness the plentiful energy that the sun naturally provides, as well as continued technology improvements and legislative frameworks that support solar power. Solar power has spread throughout various industries, revealing the route toward a future distinguished by environmental stewardship and energy resilience. This progression can be seen in everything from small rooftop installations to enormous solar farms and creative uses. When society is struggling to come to terms with the urgent need to address climate change and move away from fossil fuels, the adoption of the fundamentals of solar power appears not just as a pragmatic decision but also as a fundamental commitment to a sustainable and thriving world.

Wind Power Systems

Wind power is a strong force when it comes to the search for clean and sustainable energy resources on a worldwide scale. Wind power systems have emerged as a crucial actor in the landscape of renewable energy as the globe struggles to cope with the difficulties posed by climate change and strives to shift away from its dependency on fossil fuels. This paper investigates the fundamentals of wind power systems, including the fundamental concepts, technical breakthroughs, applications, advantages, and issues related to this transformational and unlimited energy source.

At its most fundamental level, wind power is based on the transformation of the kinetic energy present in the air's flow into electrical energy. This energy is captured by wind turbines, which are the fundamental components of wind power systems. Wind turbines are intended to transfer this energy into a form that can be utilized. The spinning of turbine blades, driven by the wind's power, is the fundamental principle that serves as the foundation. With each rotation of the blades, they provide power to a generator, transforming mechanical energy into electrical energy. Because the entire process is clean, renewable, and does not create any direct emissions of greenhouse gases while operating, wind power is an essential component of the overall effort to combat climate change anywhere in the world.

Horizontal-axis wind turbines (HAWTs) and vertical-axis wind turbines (VAWTs) are the two primary types of wind turbines developed due to technological developments in wind power systems. HAWTs are the most common variety, distinguished by their tall towers and massive blades arranged in a horizontal orientation. These wind turbines have been positioned in such a way that they face the wind, which maximizes their efficient operation. VAWTs, on the other hand, feature blades that are horizontally distributed around a central axis in a vertical orientation. Although VAWTs are less widespread than HAWTs, they have several benefits worth considering. These benefits include a straightforward design and the capacity to gather wind from any direction, making them suited for various situations.

There is a wide range of uses for wind power systems, ranging from small-scale installations not connected to the grid to large-scale wind farms used by utilities. Wind turbines of a smaller scale are frequently utilized to provide power to individual houses, farms, or distant regions where it would be impossible to connect to the grid. On the other hand, utility-scale wind farms are made up of several wind turbines deliberately positioned across huge regions to make the most of the cumulative power- generating potential. These wind farms make a substantial contribution to the global energy system. They offer a source of clean and dependable power, which helps to satisfy the growing demands of a world that needs energy.

The potential of wind power to generate electricity on a big scale is one of the characteristics distinguishing it from other forms of energy. Wind farms can generate significant quantities of power if they are located in regions with persistent and robust winds. Because of its scalability, wind power is an appealing alternative for nations and areas looking to diversify their energy mix and lessen their reliance on fossil fuels. As technology breakthroughs continue to increase the efficiency and cost-effectiveness of wind turbines, the possibility for large-scale wind power installations becomes increasingly realistic, presenting a road to a more sustainable and resilient energy future.

As the wind power sector continues to undergo fast expansion and maturation, the economic benefits of wind power are becoming increasingly apparent. Wind energy has become one of the most cost-competitive sources of electricity due to the decreasing cost of wind energy, which breakthroughs in turbine technology, manufacturing processes, and economies of scale have driven. This cost competitiveness, in conjunction with the relatively stable pricing of wind power over the long term, contributes to the attractiveness of wind power as an economically feasible energy alternative. Additionally, the wind industry is responsible for producing jobs in various fields, such as manufacture, installation, maintenance, and research and development. This helps contribute to the economy's expansion and the availability of employment possibilities in the local area.

Wind power systems are an essential component in the process of achieving greater energy independence and security. Nations and regions can reduce the risks associated with energy price volatility and geopolitical concerns by diversifying their energy mix and decreasing their reliance on limited fossil fuel supplies. The inherent decentralization of wind power aligns with the more significant trend toward distributed energy systems. This provides resilience against centralized faults and contributes to the grid's stability. In this context, wind power appears not just as an ecologically responsible option but also as a strategic decision since it promotes energy self-sufficiency and reduces susceptibility to disruptions in external energy supply.

The advantages wind power provides to the environment are substantial, and they contribute to the overarching objective of reducing the effects of climate change. While it is in operation, wind energy does not result in any direct emissions of greenhouse gases, making it a clean and renewable resource. Wind power helps lower the overall carbon footprint of energy generation by substituting conventional power sources dependent on fossil fuels. This helps to minimize air pollution. As an additional benefit, wind farms have a relatively minimal influence on land usage, which makes it possible for them to coexist with agricultural practices and other land uses. Providing habitat for particular animal species is one-way wind farms may positively influence the environment when carefully located.

Wind energy presents several obstacles, even though it offers many benefits. Wind power systems face a tremendous challenge regarding reliability because wind is characterized by its intermittent and variable nature. The generation of wind energy depends on the availability of wind and the strength of the wind, which can change frequently during the day and throughout the seasons. Considering this fluctuation, complementary solutions are required to balance supply and demand properly. When tackling these problems and assuring the continuous and dependable distribution of wind power, energy storage technologies, grid integration solutions, and innovative grid technologies are essential components.

An additional difficulty related to wind power is its possible impact on ecosystems and animals. Among the worries that detractors have mentioned include the possibility of birds and bats colliding with the blades of turbines, as well as the destruction of habitat. The installation of wind farms in locations that reduce the severity of these consequences, the execution of exhaustive environmental impact studies, and the utilization of technology such as radar systems to identify and reduce the likelihood of collisions are all critical elements in resolving these issues. It is a difficult task that requires constant study, monitoring, and collaboration among various stakeholders to find a solution that balances the demand for clean energy and biodiversity conservation.

In addition, wind farms' visual and aesthetic influence on towns and landscapes is another factor that can elicit a range of responses from affected parties. Many consider wind turbines aesthetically pleasing symbols of development and sustainability, while others may view them as eyesores that interfere with picturesque vistas. Careful planning, community interaction, and incorporating wind power projects into the larger landscape are all necessary components to strike a balance between the visual effect and the requirement for the growth of renewable energy. Public acceptability and support may be increased by effective communication and education on the advantages of wind power.

The difficulties connected with grid integration must be resolved to facilitate the expansion of wind power. Managing the variability and unpredictability of wind power becomes an essential component of grid operations as the proportion of wind energy in the total energy mix grows. Incorporating wind power into preexisting energy systems requires using several critical instruments, including demand response tactics, smart grid technology, and enhanced forecasting methodologies. In addition, increasing the flexibility and dependability of wind power integration may be accomplished by establishing regional energy markets and establishing grid links that span international borders.

When looking to the future, the research and development activities now being undertaken are centered on overcoming the problems already present and expanding the capabilities of wind power systems. Advancements have been made in turbine design, materials, and manufacturing techniques to lower prices and increase efficiency. Next-generation wind turbines, which include floating offshore turbines and airborne wind energy systems, are examples of cutting-edge technologies that can significantly enhance the potential of wind power in various geographical and environmental situations.

In conclusion, wind power systems are significant and transformational in finding clean and sustainable energy worldwide. In the future, energy generation will be divorced from the environmental and societal costs connected with current power sources based on fossil fuels. This can be accomplished by the harnessing of the wind's invisible force. The fundamentals of wind power, which include the fundamental concepts of turbine technology, as well as its numerous uses, economic advantages, and possible obstacles, highlight the relevance of wind power in the process of transitioning to an energy environment that is more robust, sustainable, and low in carbon emissions. Wind power is a beacon of hope amid the global community's combined efforts to solve the serious issues posed by climate change. Wind power exemplifies humanity's potential to harness nature's enormous and unending force to fulfill its energy requirements.

Micro-Hydro Power Generation

Micro-hydropower generation is a compelling solution that emerges as an effective solution in the search for sustainable and decentralized energy sources. This solution taps into the enormous potential of flowing water to create electricity. Micro-hydro systems provide an alternative to conventional power sources that are both renewable and kind to the environment. These systems generate electricity by harnessing the kinetic energy of rivers and streams. This essay delves into the complexities of micro-hydro power generation by examining the fundamental concepts, technical breakthroughs, environmental issues, and the transformational influence that micro-hydro power production may have on local communities and energy landscapes.

In its most fundamental form, micro-hydropower generation is based on utilizing the mechanical energy inherent in the flow of water to create electricity. Converting the kinetic energy of water into mechanical energy, which is subsequently converted into electrical energy using a generator, is the fundamental concept underpinning this technology's operation. Systems that are classified as micro-hydro are classified according to their capacity. Micro-hydro systems are often referred to as systems with a capacity ranging from a few kilowatts to one hundred kilowatts. Because of their versatility in various water sources, these systems help capture energy from different water sources, including minor rivers, streams, and even irrigation canals.

Several elements, such as the flow rate and head, which reflect the volume and vertical drop of the water source, respectively, are responsible for the design and components of a micro-hydro system. These factors are dependent on the design of the system. The fundamental elements consist of an intake structure that is responsible for redirecting water from its source, a penstock that is used to transport water to the turbine, the turbine itself, a generator that is responsible for converting mechanical energy into electricity, and a powerhouse that is used to contain and control the device. The water supply's precise features are considered when choosing the type of turbine to use. Impulse turbines, such as Pelton turbines, are ideal for high-head situations, while reaction turbines, such as Francis turbines, are suitable for medium-head settings.

Scalability is one of the distinguishing characteristics of micro-hydro power generation. This characteristic enables system customization by the available resources and the energy requirements of a specific site. Small-scale, decentralized installations allow communities to capture the energy potential of local water sources. This reduces the communities' reliance on centralized power grids and provides a stable supply of electricity in off-grid or distant locations. It is possible to implement micro-hydro systems for various uses, such as electrifying rural settlements, powering agricultural operations, and supporting small-scale companies.

The generation of power by micro-hydroelectricity has significant positive effects on the environment. Micro-hydro systems, in contrast to conventional power-generating methods that rely on fossil fuels, generate very few greenhouse gas emissions while in operation, which also helps reduce the effects of climate change. The environmental impact on aquatic ecosystems is also relatively moderate, particularly compared to more significant hydroelectric projects, including considerable dam building. This is especially true when considering comparative data. As a result of the minimal interruption to river flow and aquatic ecosystems, the natural balance of water systems is preserved, highlighting the sustainability of micro-hydro installations.

In addition to its positive effects on the environment, the generation of power through micro-hydroelectricity is in line with the principles of sustainable development since it encourages economic resilience and local participation. Micro-hydro systems act as accelerators for community development in rural and distant regions with limited access to traditional forms of power. Villages that have been electrified have higher living standards since they can have access to contemporary amenities such as lights, refrigeration, and communication gadgets. The newly discovered access to energy helps increase economic activity, assists local enterprises, and encourages entrepreneurial endeavors.

The low cost of micro-hydro systems and the ease with which they may be maintained are two factors that contribute to their widespread popularity in a variety of contexts. Micro-hydro installations need less capital investment than more significant hydropower projects. Additionally, they may frequently be developed with the participation of the community, which reduces the financial burden that more prominent hydropower projects place on governments or foreign investors. Because of the decentralized nature of these systems, energy resilience is improved. This is accomplished by reducing the transmission losses associated with centralized power grids, ultimately increasing energy delivery's overall efficiency.

Nevertheless, deploying micro-hydro power generation is accompanied by several problems and reasons to consider. During the planning phase, conducting a comprehensive analysis of site-specific aspects is necessary. These factors include considerations such as the accessibility and dependability of water supplies, geological features, and environmental impact evaluations. In addition, regulatory frameworks and approval procedures are essential in ensuring that micro-hydro projects comply with environmental legislation and community norms. It is vital to find a balance between the growth of energy and the protection of the environment to avoid unfavorable implications for the ecosystems of the immediate area and for consumers further downstream.

Micro-hydro systems need help generating continuous energy because of the intermittent water flow in rivers and streams. Seasonal fluctuations, changes in precipitation patterns, and drought conditions can all impact the dependability of these systems. As a result, it is necessary to have extra energy sources or energy storage technologies to provide a continuous power supply. Innovations in technology, such as intelligent control systems and improved forecasting methods, are being developed to address these issues and improve the efficiency of micro-hydro facilities.

Technical improvements in micro-hydro power production have increased efficiency, decreased prices, and expanded the spectrum of possible applications. Recent developments in turbine design, materials, and manufacturing methods have contributed to increased conversion efficiencies, which in turn have made it possible for micro-hydro systems to generate more power with the water resources that are now accessible.

Innovative grid technologies and remote monitoring systems improve micro-hydro installations' operational management and maintenance. This ensures that the installations work at their highest potential and resolve problems quickly.

Micro-hydro projects' success and long-term viability are directly correlated to the level of community engagement and capacity building that was implemented. Local communities' participation in the planning, implementation, and maintenance phases helps cultivate a sense of ownership and responsibility among those communities. Training programs that provide community members with the knowledge and abilities necessary for system maintenance and troubleshooting significantly contribute to the long-term survival of micro-hydroscopic systems. In addition, increasing knowledge about the advantages and disadvantages of micro-hydro power generation encourages making well-informed decisions and garners support from local stakeholders.

The landscape of micro-hydro power generation worldwide is diverse, with success stories coming from various places. For example, in Nepal, micro-hydro projects have been beneficial in delivering power to isolated mountain communities, which has significantly improved people's lives and supported commercial activity. Similarly, micro-hydro installations are helpful in countries such as Peru and Indonesia in terms of delivering energy to areas not connected to the grid and supporting efforts geared toward sustainable development. The examples shown here illustrate the versatility of micro-hydro power generation and its beneficial impact in various socio-economic and geographical situations around the world.

The role of micro-hydro power production is positioned to increase as technical breakthroughs and supporting regulations continue to improve. This is something that is expected to happen in the future. Integrating additional renewable energy sources, such as solar and wind, provides a hybrid approach to creating energy. This method combines the advantages of many technologies to improve the dependability and efficiency of the electricity-generating process. Technological advancements in energy storage have been made to solve the issue of intermittency and contribute to the stability of micro-hydro systems. These technologies include batteries and pumped storage.

In conclusion, the generation of power through micro-hydroelectricity is a solution that is both promising and varied when it comes to the search for energy sources that are both sustainable and decentralized. Micro-hydro devices can capture the kinetic energy of flowing water to provide communities with a dependable and ecologically beneficial source of electricity. Micro-hydroelectricity is an appealing choice for rural electrification because of its scalability, affordability, and minimum environmental impact. It also helps to sustain local businesses and fosters a sense of empowerment. Micro-hydropower generation is becoming an increasingly important factor in the formation of a resilient and equitable energy future as the globe works toward the transition toward energy solutions that are cleaner and more sustainable.

CHAPTER IV

Water Harvesting and Purification

Rainwater Harvesting

Rainwater harvesting, an age-old tradition, has recently come into the spotlight as a viable and practical alternative to fulfill the growing demand for water in the face of escalating environmental issues and increasing water scarcity. Harvesting rainwater is an example of a comprehensive approach to water management since it allows for utilizing rainfall's plentiful and unutilized resources. This paper aims to investigate the fundamentals of rainwater collection, including its historical origins, technological elements, applications, advantages, and obstacles. Rainwater harvesting is emerging as a straightforward yet effective way to preserve water, boost resilience, and build a more sustainable future. This is something that is becoming increasingly important as civilizations all over the world struggle with the necessity of sustainable resource usage.

The practice of collecting rainwater has been around for millennia, and historical evidence of its practices can be found in a variety of civilizations all around the world. The practice of collecting and storing rainwater has been around for a very long time. Ancient civilizations such as the Romans used it to build sophisticated aqueducts and cisterns to collect rainfall. Additionally, populations in dry regions have employed traditional rainwater tanks. Over the last several decades, there has been a resurgence in rainwater collection, which has become an essential component of sustainable water management techniques.

This is due to the intensification of water shortages and climate change worries.

Gathering and storing rainwater for later use is the fundamental premise of rainwater harvesting, also known as rainwater collecting. This may be accomplished by utilizing a wide range of methods and technologies, ranging from straightforward and time-honored approaches to complex and cutting-edge systems. One of the most frequent methods is roof-based harvesting, which involves collecting rainwater that falls on rooftops by directing it via gutters and into storage containers. Surface runoff harvesting from landscapes, such as roadways and catchment areas, and subsurface harvesting, which involves collecting rainfall from subterranean sources, are two more approaches that can be utilized.

The technological elements of rainwater harvesting systems include various components meant to collect, store, and distribute rainwater efficiently. Catchment systems for roofs typically consist of gutters, downspouts, and leaf screens. These components are designed to collect and filter rainwater as it travels down the roof. A variety of storage devices, such as tanks and cisterns, are meant to retain the collected rainwater. These systems have capacities that vary to satisfy varied levels of demand. First-flush devices and filters remove impurities and debris from the initial discharge. This helps to guarantee that the retained water is of high quality. The transportation of rainwater for various purposes, including irrigation, landscaping, and even as a source of drinking water after it has been adequately treated, can be accomplished through distribution systems that may include pumps, pipelines, and controllers.

The gathering of rainwater has a wide range of uses, including those in the home, agricultural, industrial, and communal settings. Rainwater collected can be used in residential settings to facilitate activities such as irrigation, flushing toilets, and washing and complement or replace traditional water sources. In agriculture, rainwater collection offers an alternate water supply for agricultural irrigation, decreasing dependency on groundwater or surface water sources running out. Rainwater harvesting may benefit industries because it allows them to profit from the gathered water by using it for activities that do not need potable water quality. This helps to reduce the burden that is placed on municipal water sources. Increase the amount of available water by installing rainwater collecting systems at the community level. This is especially beneficial in areas that are experiencing water shortages or have water infrastructure that could be more trustworthy.

One of the most significant benefits of rainwater collecting is its contribution to the preservation of water and the preservation of the environment. The ability of communities to considerably reduce their reliance on conventional water supplies may be accomplished by collecting rainwater, which is frequently neglected and allowed to stream freely. The principles of sustainable water management are adhered to by this approach, which encourages the effective utilization of available water resources and reduces the negative influence on the environment that is often connected with the extraction of water from rivers, lakes, or aquifers. Through the reduction of the demand for water from sensitive habitats and the mitigation of the consequences of water extraction on aquatic ecosystems, rainwater collection contributes to the preservation of natural ecosystems.

Collecting rainwater is naturally decentralized, which grants individuals, households, and communities the ability to operate independently in managing their water resources. The diversification of water sources and the reduction of dependency on centralized water delivery systems are two ways in which this decentralization brings increased resilience. In areas with insufficient or unreliable conventional water infrastructure, rainwater collection emerges as a dependable and easily accessible water supply. As an additional benefit, the flexibility of rainwater collecting systems enables scalability, enabling communities to modify their solutions to meet their area's specific water requirements and the existing environmental circumstances.

There are several different ways in which rainwater gathering yields economic benefits. Both individuals and governments can experience cost savings due to the decreased demand for centralized water delivery systems and the related investment in infrastructure. Gathering rainwater can improve crop yields and minimize dependency on expensive irrigation systems or purchased water. Rainwater harvesting is particularly useful in agriculture, where water is an essential input. Industries that collect rainwater may realize financial benefits by utilizing gathered water for operations that do not require potable water. This eliminates the need for costly water treatment or the disposal of effluent.

Rainwater harvesting is a sustainable stormwater management approach that may be used in urban environments characterized by impervious surfaces such as roads and buildings that contribute to creating urban floods and stormwater runoff. Reducing the amount and intensity of stormwater flow can be accomplished by the collection and storage of rainfall, which in turn reduces the likelihood of floods and soil erosion. An additional benefit of this approach is that it helps replenish local groundwater aquifers, contributing to urban water systems' general health and sustainability.

Collecting rainwater helps improve water quality by lowering the amount of pollution that occurs in natural water sources. Pollutants, including oil, heavy metals, and pesticides, are frequently carried by stormwater runoff in urban contexts, negatively impacting rivers and lakes. It is possible to prevent the introduction of these contaminants into natural water bodies through rainwater harvesting, which involves redirecting and collecting rainfall before it becomes runoff. Furthermore, the filtering and treatment procedures built into rainwater harvesting systems guarantee that the retained water will continue to be of high quality and acceptable for various applications without the need for significant chemical treatments.

Rainwater collection has several social advantages, including better water availability and resilience, particularly in marginalized or neglected populations. There is still a severe problem in many regions of the world about the availability of clean and dependable water. To circumvent the significant and expensive water infrastructure requirement, rainwater collecting provides a decentralized option that may be deployed at the home or community level. This empowerment helps to build community involvement, self-reliance, and a sense of ownership over water resources, all of which contribute to the general well-being of communities.

Rainwater harvesting, despite the many benefits it offers, has its share of obstacles, which should be taken into mind. Regarding the efficiency of rainwater collecting systems, the quantity and consistency of rainfall are two of the most important factors to consider. The possibility of feasible rainwater collection may be restricted to dry or semi-arid locations with either inconsistent or infrequent rainfall. In addition, climate change brings about unpredictability in the patterns of rainfall, which may affect the dependability of rainwater as a reliable water supply. To make the most of the benefits that rainwater collecting offers, it is necessary to undergo adequate planning and evaluate the local climate.

Worries over the purity of the water additionally complicate the gathering of rainwater. Initial runoff from roofs or catchment surfaces may contain dust, bird droppings, or atmospheric pollutants. These contaminants may be present in the runoff of these surfaces. This problem may be solved by installing efficient first-flush devices and filters; nevertheless, it is essential to perform routine maintenance to guarantee that the collected rainwater will continue to be high quality. Furthermore, additional measures may be required to protect water quality in urban contexts, where rooftops may be vulnerable to contamination from industrial operations or airborne pollutants. This is because roofs are more likely to be contaminated by pollution.

One of the potential obstacles to the broad adoption of rainwater collecting systems is the initial expense of constructing these systems, which is especially problematic in economically disadvantaged regions. However, the initial expenditure may be difficult for people or groups with little financial means, although rainwater collecting is often cost-effective over the long run. To overcome this obstacle and encourage the broad use of rainwater collecting, the government may provide financial incentives, subsidies, or financing based on community development.

In conclusion, rainwater collecting is a solution that is both sustainable and multidimensional, with the potential to alleviate water scarcity, develop resilience, and contribute to the protection of the environment. Its relevance is highlighted within the framework of environmentally responsible water management because it has historical origins, technological elements, a wide range of uses, and several advantages. The global community is grappling with the interconnected challenges of population growth, climate change, and environmental degradation. Rainwater harvesting is a strategy that is both practical and accessible, and it invites individuals, communities, and nations to become water stewards, thereby cultivating a more sustainable and water-secure future.

Well Digging and Maintenance

Since ancient times, wells have been essential water sources, giving populations a dependable and dispersed way to obtain this vital resource. The process of drilling wells and the following upkeep of these installations are essential to guarantee a reliable and sustainable water supply. This paper explores the foundations of sound excavation and the technological features, historical background, and importance of healthy maintenance. Understanding good building and maintenance becomes essential as civilizations struggle with water shortages and strive for water security, public health, and community resilience.

The history of well-drilling is closely linked to the search for water by human civilization. Groundwater availability was vital to ancient societies, and drilling wells was a revolutionary deed that promoted agriculture, urbanization, and established populations. Construction changed over time, moving from crude hand-dug wells to more advanced techniques using machines and tools. Wells became lifelines, giving local populations a consistent and confined supply of water—a practice that still exists today.

The technological elements of sound excavation comprise an array of techniques and instruments tailored to the geological circumstances, water table level, and the well's intended purpose. The manual excavation process for hand-dug wells, still used in many areas, involves shovels and buckets. Auger drilling is used to drill holes into the Earth, especially where the soil is softer. Rotary drilling—

which uses a revolving drill bit driven by machinery—is an efficient technique to penetrate more authoritarian rock formations—furthermore, percussive drilling breaks through subterranean materials with repeated hits. The depth of the water table, available resources, and geological factors all play a role in determining which approach is best.

For these water sources to remain safe and functioning, well upkeep is necessary. Ignoring well upkeep can result in contamination risk, structural problems, and a deterioration in water quality. Well-maintenance includes routine inspections, cleaning, repairs, and adherence to hygienic procedures. Periodic examinations, usually carried out by experts or qualified personnel, assess the state of the well casing, screens, and pump parts. Any indications of wear or damage are quickly fixed to avert more severe problems.

The importance of drilling and maintaining wells goes beyond providing instant access to water; it also has broader consequences for community development, environmental sustainability, and public health. One crucial factor determining public health is consistent access to clean water. By guaranteeing a clean and safe water supply, wells built and maintained correctly help avoid illnesses spread by polluted water. Because contaminants like chemicals, germs, and viruses can enter wells through various openings, routine maintenance, and inspections are essential to protecting the public's health.

Digging wells is a socio-economic development catalyst in the field of community development. It takes less time and effort to gather water when there is a close, dependable supply available, especially for women and children, who typically do this. These time savings make increased educational possibilities, economic activity, and general communal well-being possible. Wells plays a crucial role in agricultural settings by facilitating irrigation, improving crop yields, and promoting food security.

Ecological sustainability is intrinsically connected to conscientious, sound excavation and upkeep procedures. Care must be taken while managing wells that draw from groundwater reservoirs to prevent over-extraction and aquifer depletion. Groundwater resources and the delicate balance of aquifer ecosystems are protected when wells are designed, positioned, and maintained correctly. A thorough grasp of the hydrogeological characteristics in the area, the demand for water, and the possible environmental effects of well building are all necessary for sustainable well management.

Digging and maintaining wells are especially important in areas with limited water supplies or unstable surface water sources. Wells can be used to access groundwater, which is kept in aquifers under the surface of the Earth. In dry and semi-arid areas with scarce surface water, wells serve as vital resources for agriculture and society. However, sustainable groundwater exploitation depends on appropriate methods to prevent depletion and guarantee the durability of this essential resource.

Collaboration between several stakeholders, such as communities, governments, non-governmental organizations, and technical specialists, is necessary for well-digging initiatives to be successful. The sense of ownership and responsibility fostered by local knowledge and involvement makes community involvement essential to the sustainability of promising initiatives. Governments are involved in regulating well building, enforcing safety regulations, and promoting environmentally friendly water management techniques. Non-governmental groups are frequently essential to financing and executing good projects, particularly in areas with few resources.

Digging and maintaining wells also require a deep understanding of the hydrogeological and geological conditions unique to each site. The level of the water table, the pace at which aquifers recharge, and the possibility of groundwater pollution are all determined by hydrogeological evaluations. The selection of suitable well-building techniques and materials is guided by the characterization of subsurface materials, aided by geophysical surveys and borehole logging.

Hydrogeological studies are used to choose an appropriate location, which is the first step in the well-building process. The area's geology, the well's intended purpose, and the depth of the water table all influence the type of well and the chosen construction technique. Hand-dug wells, prevalent in many areas, are excavated by hand with shovels and buckets. Although these wells are manual, they are frequently more practical in regions with softer soils. On the other hand, drilling wells employ equipment to dig through the Earth and reach the water table, such augers or rotary drills. Variables, including the kind of soil, the level of the water table, and the accessible resources, impact the decision between these approaches.

Drilling or digging a borehole, adding a casing to keep it from collapsing, and adding screens to filter out silt while letting water in are standard steps in the building process. The gravel packing surrounding the screens increases the efficiency of the well, which keeps small particles out. Preventing surface water from entering the well is part of a proper sound design since it might bring pollutants. The well is covered to keep out trash, insects, and other possible sources of pollution. The last phase is installing a pump to raise the water to the surface for distribution.

After a well is built, routine upkeep becomes crucial.

Regular inspections include examining the wellhead, casing, and visible parts. We check the pump and related equipment for wear and malfunctions. Periodic water quality testing is done to make sure the healthy water satisfies safety requirements. If problems are found during inspections, they must be fixed right away to stop more contamination and degradation.

Common problems like biofouling, or the accumulation of biological material that can clog screens and lower well efficiency, must also be addressed as part of good maintenance. Groundwater frequently contains deposits of iron and manganese, which can cause discoloration and bad smells. Periodic disinfection is necessary due to the possibility of bacterial contamination. To preserve the quality of the water, it is essential to stop the entrance of foreign materials or items into the well.

Well rehabilitation may eventually be necessary in addition to periodic maintenance to restore the well's production. Cleaning the well, clearing out deposits or silt buildup, and fixing or replacing broken parts are all part of rehabilitation. Rehabilitation work aims to increase good performance and prolong its useful life.

Upkeep involves more than just technical concerns; it also involves socio-economic and cultural factors. Programs for well upkeep must include community involvement and education. The local community must understand the necessity of good maintenance, how to spot any problems and the procedures that prolong well life and improve water quality.

Wells are frequently essential for maintaining communities and agriculture in areas with limited surface water supplies or scarce water resources. Groundwater is a dependable and dispersed water supply kept in aquifers under the surface of the Earth. In dry and semi-arid areas with low surface water, wells serve as vital resources for agriculture and society. However, sustainable groundwater exploitation depends on appropriate methods to prevent depletion and guarantee the durability of this essential resource.

Collaboration between several stakeholders, such as communities, governments, non-governmental organizations, and technical specialists, is necessary for well-digging initiatives to be successful. The sense of ownership and responsibility fostered by local knowledge and involvement makes community involvement essential to the sustainability of promising initiatives. Governments are involved in regulating well building, enforcing safety regulations, and promoting environmentally friendly water management techniques. Non-governmental groups are frequently essential to financing and executing good projects, particularly in areas with few resources.

Digging and maintaining wells also require a deep understanding of the hydrogeological and geological conditions unique to each site. The level of the water table, the pace at which aquifers recharge, and the possibility of groundwater pollution are all determined by hydrogeological evaluations. The selection of suitable well-building techniques and materials is guided by the characterization of subsurface materials, aided by geophysical surveys and borehole logging.

Hydrogeological studies are used to choose an appropriate location, which is the first step in the well-building process. The area's geology, the well's intended purpose, and the depth of the water table all influence the type of well and the chosen construction technique. Hand-dug wells, prevalent in many areas, are excavated by hand with shovels and buckets. Although these wells are manual, they are frequently more practical in regions with softer soils. On the other hand, drilling wells employ equipment to dig through the Earth and reach the water table, such augers or rotary drills. Variables, including the kind of soil, the level of the water table, and the accessible resources, impact the decision between these approaches.

Drilling or digging a borehole, adding a casing to keep it from collapsing, and adding screens to filter out silt while letting water in are standard steps in the building process. The gravel packing surrounding the screens increases the efficiency of the well, which keeps small particles out. Preventing surface water from entering the well is part of a proper sound design since it might bring pollutants. The well is covered to keep out trash, insects, and other possible sources of pollution. The last phase is installing a pump to raise the water to the surface for distribution. After a well is built, routine upkeep becomes crucial.

Regular inspections include examining the wellhead, casing, and visible parts. We check the pump and related equipment for wear and malfunctions. Periodic water quality testing is done to make sure the well water satisfies safety requirements. If problems are found during inspections, they must be fixed right away to stop more contamination and degradation.

Common problems like biofouling, or the accumulation of biological material that can clog screens and lower well efficiency, must also be addressed as part of good maintenance. Groundwater frequently contains deposits of iron and manganese, which can cause discoloration and bad smells. Periodic disinfection is necessary due to the possibility of bacterial contamination. To preserve the quality of the water, it is essential to stop the entrance of foreign materials or items into the well.

Well rehabilitation may eventually be necessary in addition to periodic maintenance to restore the well's production. Cleaning the well, clearing out deposits or silt buildup, and fixing or replacing broken parts are all part of rehabilitation. Rehabilitation work aims to increase good performance and prolong its useful life.

Upkeep involves more than just technical concerns; it also involves socio-economic and cultural factors. Programs for well upkeep must include community involvement and education. The local community must understand the necessity of good maintenance, how to spot any problems and the procedures that prolong well life and improve water quality.

In summary, well construction and upkeep are essential elements of sustainable water management that support environmental sustainability, community growth, and public health. The fact that wells have been used as water sources for so long emphasizes their importance. To ensure that people have access to clean, dependable water as societies deal with the problems of water scarcity, climate change, and population increase, well-digging and well-maintenance methods become crucial. When done correctly and with a knowledge of the local environment, well digging may be a tool for community empowerment, resilience, and preserving a priceless resource essential to life and livelihoods.

CHAPTER V

Sustainable Agriculture

Off-Grid Gardening Basics

Off-grid gardening is becoming an increasingly important component in the quest for sustainable living since it allows people and communities to raise their own food in a self-sufficient manner. This paper aims to investigate the fundamental concepts of off-grid gardening. It will explore the essential practices, concerns, and benefits of maintaining a garden independent of regular utilities. It is becoming more critical for those interested in living a more sustainable and independent lifestyle to understand off-grid gardening. This is because the globe faces environmental difficulties and the necessity for robust, decentralized computer systems.

Growing plants without relying on centralized water, energy, or heating systems is the essence of off-grid gardening. This is not to be confused with conventional gardening. According to the concepts of self-sufficiency, environmental stewardship, and the aspiration for more autonomy in food production, this strategy is consistent with those objectives. The fundamentals of off-grid gardening include a variety of aspects, such as the management of water, the sources of energy, the health of the soil, and the selection of plants, respectively.

Off-grid gardening is based on the principle that water is a valuable resource and essential to manage water resources effectively. Off-grid gardeners typically rely on rainwater gathering, wells, or other local water sources because they need access to city water supply. A water supply that is both sustainable and decentralized may be created by collecting rainwater from rooftops and storing it in storage tanks. Through the utilization of drip irrigation or soaker hoses, well-designed irrigation systems contribute to maximizing water efficiency and reducing water waste. In addition, choosing plants that are resistant to drought and suitable for the location contributes to water saving in off-grid gardening.

Especially in areas where typical grid electricity is not accessible, the importance of energy sources for off-grid gardening cannot be overstated. Solar power is an environmentally friendly alternative since it may supply energy for activities such as pumping water, operating irrigation systems, or powering greenhouse operations. Off-grid gardeners can use photovoltaic panels and solar-powered water pumps to capture the sun's energy for various gardening requirements. The energy sustainability of off-grid gardening may be further improved by investing in energy-efficient equipment and applying passive solar design ideas to greenhouse structures.

The health of the soil is of the utmost importance for practical off-grid gardening since it directly influences the development and production of plants. One of the most essential practices in off-grid gardening is composting, which is converting organic waste into nutrient-rich compost that enhances the structure and richness of the soil. Mulching is another vital practice that provides a protective coating on the top of the soil. This layer helps store moisture, reduce weeds, and improve the soil's overall health. Those who garden off the grid frequently emphasize organic and regenerative methods, avoiding synthetic fertilizers and pesticides to foster a more natural and environmentally responsible approach to gardening.

In off-grid gardening, one of the most important things to consider is the selection of appropriate plant kinds.

Gardeners can store seeds from year to year by selecting heirloom and open-pollinated seeds. This helps gardeners become more self-sufficient and maintains the diversity of plant species. When you choose native or adapted plant species, you not only ensure that they are more resistant to the temperature conditions of the area, but you also limit the amount of significant inputs that are required, such as water and fertilizers. Crop rotation and companion planting are two more tactics utilized in off- grid gardening to maximize the health of plants and reduce the likelihood of being affected by diseases and pests.

When gardening off the grid, it is common practice to adjust one's practices to the seasons' natural cycles and the area's climate. To design and manage a successful off-grid garden, it is vital to have a solid understanding of the growth seasons, the dates of frost, and the temperature changes. Off-grid gardeners can develop crops outside the traditional growing season by utilizing cold frames, greenhouses, and other season-extending constructions. This results in an increase in the total output of the garden. In addition, the adoption of permaculture principles, including the design of polyculture systems and the incorporation of perennial plants, helps the sustainability and resilience of off-grid gardening.

Beyond the immediate availability of fresh, homegrown vegetables, gardening has further advantages outside the grid. Individuals and communities are given the ability to take charge of their food supply, which is one of the most significant advantages. Individuals can lessen their dependency on external food supplies and the industrial agriculture system by engaging in off-grid gardening, which helps cultivate self-sufficiency. This independence is beneficial when the economy is unstable; there are interruptions in food supply networks or limited access to traditional utilities.

Off-grid gardening is based on environmental sustainability as its guiding premise. Off-grid gardeners contribute to decreasing their ecological footprint by reducing their dependency on centralized water and electricity sources as much as possible. It aligns with broader environmental aims emphasizing organic techniques, soil health, and water conservation. This promotes a more regenerative and environmentally sound approach to food production. Localized and resilient food systems that emphasize environmental stewardship might be modeled after off-grid gardening, which serves as a model for such systems.

By cultivating a profound connection to the natural world, off-grid gardening encourages individuals to interact with the natural cycles that occur throughout the year and the changing seasons. Culturing an excellent appreciation for the complexities of plant life and the ecosystems that sustain it may be accomplished via the practical experience of growing food from seed to harvest. This connection to nature brings about personal fulfillment and contributes to a more significant societal movement toward living more considerate and environmentally responsible.

Off-grid gardening is vital for several reasons, including its social elements. It is common for communities that engage in off-grid gardening to join together to share their expertise, resources, and the bounty of their crops. Community gardens, whether in urban or rural areas, offer spaces for communal cultivation, which helps to strengthen social relationships and encourages a sense of shared responsibility for the provision of food. Through the sharing of seeds, plants, and gardening practices, a cultural enrichment is created, which strengthens the community's resilience and cohesiveness.

Off-grid gardening presents difficulties, which require innovative solutions and flexible methods. Gardeners not connected to the grid may have problems due to limited access to water or changes in the water supply. This highlights the need for water-efficient practices and careful planning. Off-grid gardeners may need to adopt extra tactics to protect plants and maximize growth conditions in locations that experience severe temperatures, such as sweltering summers or frigid winters. Off-grid gardeners are compelled to investigate natural and holistic methods of plant health since controlling pests and diseases without synthetic pesticides can be a steep learning curve.

It is necessary to have access to resources and information for off-grid gardening projects to be successful. It may be beneficial for communities or people new to off-grid gardening to participate in training programs, workshops, and mentorship opportunities to become proficient in the essential skills and knowledge. It is also possible to build outlets for exchanging information and assistance within the community of off-grid gardeners by engaging in online forums, joining local gardening clubs, or networking with experienced off-grid gardeners.

Off-grid gardening stands out as a concrete and accessible approach for individuals to embrace a more self-sufficient and ecologically conscious lifestyle. This has become increasingly popular as the interest in sustainable living and off-grid activities continues to develop. Off-grid gardening provides a means of reestablishing a connection with the earth, lessening the influence on the environment, and fostering resilience in the face of external uncertainty. This can be accomplished in urban roofs, suburban plots, or rural homesteads. Individuals and communities can begin on a journey toward sustainable, regenerative, and fulfilling food production by adopting the fundamentals of off-grid gardening. These fundamentals include water and energy management, soil health, plant selection, and community participation. Through their actions, individuals contribute to a broader movement that envisions a future in which gardening becomes a source of nourishment and a transforming force for good change.

Permaculture Techniques

As a comprehensive and regenerative approach to planning human settlements and food production systems, permaculture, which is a mashup of the words "permanent" and "agriculture" or "culture," is a concept that has gained popularity in recent years. Bill Mollison and David Holmgren may have conceived the idea of permaculture in the 1970s. Still, it has since developed into a worldwide movement that adheres to environmentally responsible and sustainable principles. To create harmonious, resilient, and self-sufficient habitats, the fundamental goal of permaculture is to create surroundings similar to the patterns and interactions found in natural ecosystems. This article aims to investigate the wide variety of permaculture approaches that serve as the basis for this ecological design system. These techniques include sustainable agriculture, water management, soil fertility, and community development methods.

Permaculture concepts are profoundly based on monitoring and receiving knowledge from natural ecosystems. Permaculturists are interested in designing human systems that can blend in seamlessly with the natural environment. They do this by understanding the complex interactions between plants, animals, soil, water, and climate. Permaculture is centered on sustainable agriculture, and one of the most essential techniques utilized is the establishment of food forests or forest gardens. A wide range of fruit and nut trees, shrubs, herbs, and ground-cover plants are some of the components included in food forests. These forests are designed to mimic the structure and function of natural forests. The lofty canopy trees, which provide shade and habitat; the understory plants, which contribute to biodiversity; and the ground-cover plants, which preserve the soil and prevent erosion, are all examples of layers that each perform a distinct role in the ecosystem. This multi-layered method allows for maximum output while simultaneously reducing the amount of required external inputs, such as synthetic fertilizers and pesticides.

Within the permaculture framework, "guilds" are essential to sustainable agriculture. When a collection of plants and animals collaborate in a mutually beneficial way, they are referred to as a guild. Each guild member contributes to the system's general health and production. As an illustration, a guild of fruit trees may include plants that fix nitrogen to improve soil fertility, plants that are dynamic accumulators to bring minerals up from deeper soil layers, and plants that are pest-repellent to prevent harmful insects from entering the soil. The resilience and efficiency that can be seen in natural ecosystems are reflected in the diversity and complexity of guilds. In natural ecosystems, diverse species work together to benefit all of them.

Another essential component of permaculture design is the management of water resources. Rainwater collection and storage have become necessary methods in areas characterized by dry and semi-arid conditions. A reduction in dependency on centralized water supplies can be achieved by the process of rainwater harvesting, which includes collecting and storing rainwater for later use. Techniques include the installation of rainwater collection systems on rooftops, the construction of swales (contour trenches) to slow down water flow and increase infiltration, and the construction of earthworks such as ponds or cisterns to store rainwater that has been collected. The practitioners of permaculture also highlight the significance of using water effectively through methods such as mulching, which helps prevent evaporation; drip irrigation, which directs water to the roots of plants; and the selection of plant kinds that can withstand drought.

Permaculture concentrates on increasing the fertility of the soil via the application of regenerative methods, which is complementary to water management. Cover crops or green manure is a critical approach that may be utilized. These plants develop quickly and are subsequently absorbed into the soil to improve the structure of the soil, contribute organic matter, and increase the levels of nutrients. Cover crops are the best way to stop soil erosion, control weed growth, and produce a living mulch that shields the soil from the damaging effects of temperature fluctuations. Creating a garden bed that does not require digging can also be accomplished by using sheet mulching or lasagna gardening, which involves layers of organic materials such as cardboard, straw, and compost. This is a simulation of the natural decomposition process, which helps maintain the soil's structure and vitality.

Permaculture emphasizes the significance of developing closed-loop systems that reduce waste while maximizing resource utilization. Composting is a fundamental method that converts organic waste into nutrient-rich humus. This is accomplished by completing the nutrient cycle and decreasing the need for fertilizers obtained from outside sources. In vermiculture, also known as worm composting, earthworms break down organic matter into rich castings, producing a beneficial soil amendment. Vermiculture is an extension of this methodology. In addition, bio-intensive gardening strategies, such as crop rotation and companion planting, maximize space and nutrients while reducing the likelihood of pests and illnesses.

An integrated land-use management system combining trees and shrubs with crops and animals is an example of agroforestry, which embodies permaculture concepts. Agroforestry offers many advantages, including the enhancement of soil fertility, the enhancement of biodiversity, and the enhancement of resilience to climate fluctuations. These advantages are achieved by imitating the ecosystems of natural forests. A prominent method of agroforestry that increases the efficiency with which land is utilized is called alley cropping. Alley cropping involves planting rows of trees or shrubs with crops grown between them. Silvopasture is a kind of farming that combines trees, fodder, and livestock in a mutually beneficial system. This method offers shade for animals, grass for grazing, and the production of lumber or fruit from trees.

The concept of permaculture encompasses the physical components of land management and the social and community aspects of environmental management. In the field of social permaculture, which is becoming increasingly popular, the primary focus is on developing human systems that encourage collaboration, communication, and resilience. In permaculture, community-building tactics include creating shared spaces, communal gardens, and cooperative ventures. These approaches are designed to develop social relationships and inspire collective responsibility for living sustainably. The design of eco-villages, intentional communities, and regenerative urban areas that promote ecological resilience, energy efficiency, and social harmony are all examples of how permaculture principles may be applied to human settlements.

One of the most important aspects of permaculture is the realization that every system component serves several purposes and that several other components support each function. This idea, referred to as "stacking functions," guarantees that every design element contributes to the system's overall effectiveness and robustness. As an illustration, a fruit tree in a permaculture design not only supplies food but also provides shade, encourages biodiversity, contributes to soil fertility, and works as a windbreak. With this multifunctional approach, the productive capacity of each component within the system is maximized to its total capability.

Techniques used in permaculture are versatile and adaptive and are meant to meet the particular requirements and conditions of a given destination. A comprehensive observation and analysis of the land's natural components, climate, and geography is the first step in the process. Eventually, a permaculture design will develop, which will include a variety of methods and components into a consistent and sustainable system. When designing a landscape, it is essential to consider the patterns of water flow, the direction of the wind, the amount of sunshine exposure, and the microclimates to maximize the placement of components within the landscape.

In conclusion, the permaculture approaches reflect a paradigm change in how we approach land management, agriculture, and communal life. The permaculture philosophy, founded on ecological principles and a profound reverence for the natural world, provides a comprehensive framework for designing regenerative systems that benefit both people and the environment. Permaculture approaches offer a blueprint for creating resilient, self-sufficient, and harmonious systems that align with the broader aims of sustainability and ecological stewardship. These techniques may be applied to backyard gardens, small-scale farms, or large-scale landscapes. As more and more people and communities become aware of the need to reestablish our connection to the planet, permaculture serves as a guiding light, pointing us in the direction of a future in which our activities are in harmony with the natural world, therefore creating plenty, variety, and long-term sustainability.

CHAPTER VI

Waste Management Solutions

Composting for Off-Grid Living

Composting is a fundamental component of off-grid living, which is centered around the goal of being self-sufficient and environmentally conscious. Composting is a vital technique for creating nutrient-rich soil without outside assistance. Organic waste may be turned into a valuable soil amendment through the natural, cyclical process of composting, which completes the nutrient cycle and promotes sustainable agriculture. Composting becomes essential while living off the grid, as access to artificial fertilizers and centralized waste disposal may be restricted. The complexities of composting for off-grid living are examined in this article, along with the science underlying the procedure, several approaches to composting, and the broader effects of integrating composting into a sustainable way of life.

Microorganisms control the biological process of composting, which transforms organic matter into humus—a nutrient-rich, crumbly black material. This process happens organically in ecosystems when plant detritus, fallen leaves, and other organic matter break down and replenish the soil with nutrients. Composting intentionally speeds up and leverages this natural decomposition process to provide a nutrient-rich soil conditioner in off-grid living situations. Browns and greens are commonly referred to as the essential components for a successful composting process. Greens are nitrogen-rich materials like manure, fresh yard waste, and kitchen scraps, while browns are carbon-rich materials like straw, dried leaves, and shredded newspaper. For the composting process to be optimized, these elements must be balanced.

A straightforward, small-scale compost heap or container may be made to compost while living off the grid. This approach calls for layering alternate browns and greens to promote decomposition, ensuring sufficient aeration, and periodically stirring the compost. The cooperative efforts of fungus, bacteria, and other microorganisms that flourish in the warm, aerobic environment aid the composting heap. These microbes break down the organic materials over time, producing heat as a byproduct. In addition to quickening the decomposition process, this heat is essential in eliminating pathogens and weed seeds, making a safe compost full of nutrients. Vermicomposting, sometimes known as worm composting, is an additional well-liked off-grid method that breaks down organic waste by using earthworms. This procedure introduces redworms (Eisenia fetida or Eisenia andrei) into a specified worm bin. These worms consume organic items such as kitchen trash. The worms break down the organic stuff into nutrient-rich castings as they eat it. Vermicomposting is an excellent option for off-grid living because it takes up less room, doesn't smell bad, and can handle kitchen waste effectively. The resultant worm castings, sometimes called "black gold," are an effective organic soil conditioner and fertilizer.

A valuable option for more extensive off-grid areas is the three-bin composting system. This method allows for a sequential composting process consisting of three adjacent units. Fresh organic materials are placed in the first bin, materials in the active decomposition phase are placed in the second bin, and completed compost ready for use is placed in the third bin. This method offers a consistent supply of nutrient-rich compost for farming or gardening by enabling an ongoing compost cycle.

Waste disposal in isolated or off-grid areas is addressed with composting toilets, a novel off-grid use of composting. These toilets do away with the requirement for conventional sewage systems by using aerobic decomposition to convert human waste into compost. To facilitate decomposition, carbon-rich materials (such as sawdust or coconut coir) are added, and the composting process is given enough time to complete. The produced compost may be safely applied to non-edible landscaping, completing the ecologically responsible human waste treatment cycle.

Composting has several advantages that go well beyond just instantly creating soil that is rich in nutrients. Composting is consistent with the off-grid lifestyle tenets of ecological stewardship, resource conservation, and sustainability. The environmental effect of off-grid living is minimized since organic waste may be recycled on-site, reducing the need for outside trash disposal services. Composting also helps to reduce greenhouse gas emissions by reducing methane emissions that would otherwise result from landfills' anaerobic decomposition processes.

This procedure results in nutrient-rich compost, a potent organic fertilizer that improves plant development and soil fertility. Compost gives soil structure and a balanced mix of vital nutrients, unlike commercial fertilizers that can include dangerous chemicals and pollute water. This is especially helpful for off-grid farming operations since it reduces dependency on outside resources and emphasizes self-sufficiency.

Regenerative agriculture is a comprehensive agricultural method that aims to improve soil health, biodiversity, and ecosystem resilience. Composting is in line with these goals. Small-scale farming or homesteading are common aspects of off-grid life, and the fertility of the soil directly affects the productivity of agricultural pursuits. As a soil conditioner, compost enhances nutrient availability, aeration, and water retention. Composting helps to create a regenerative and self-sustaining agricultural system that aligns with the ideals of off-grid life.

Including composting in off-grid living methods also promotes a closer relationship with life's natural cycles. People who participate in the composting process get to see personally how yard trash and food scraps are converted into an invaluable resource for the soil. Encouraging accountability and attention, this cyclical approach to waste management strengthens the idea that organic matter is not garbage but an essential component of the greater ecosystem.

Education and community involvement are essential when it comes to encouraging composting habits in off-grid living environments. Community projects, training courses, and workshops may give people the information and abilities to set up efficient composting systems. Off-grid residents can work together to manage organic waste and share the compost that results by setting up shared composting sites or community composting hubs. This collaborative method improves the fabric of off-grid communities and highlights the benefits of composting in a larger sense.

Composting for off-grid life has many benefits, but it also has drawbacks. The correct ratio of greens to browns, sufficient moisture retention, and adequate aeration are all necessary for composting to be successful. Sustaining compost in off-grid areas with limited water access may depend on careful monitoring and management of moisture levels. Furthermore, composting takes time, so those waiting for organic matter to be transformed into nutrient-rich compost must exercise patience.

Composting for off-grid living is a perfect example of sustainable, regenerative living that puts the environment's needs and self-sufficiency first. The many composting techniques, ranging from small-scale compost heaps to vermicomposting systems and community composting projects, provide adaptable options for people and groups looking to develop nutrient- rich soil in balance with the environment. Composting is a practical and approachable method consistent with the ideals of off-grid living, especially in light of the global environmental issues and growing emphasis on sustainable living. Composting is an excellent way for off- grid people to manage their organic waste and help create resilient, regenerative ecosystems that are the cornerstone of sustainable and peaceful life.

Recycling and Upcycling

The ideas of recycling and upcycling have become essential components of sustainability due to the growing worries about the environment and the increasing difficulty of managing garbage. By turning trash into valuable resources and promoting a more circular economy, these methods show creative ways to reduce waste reduction. Recycling is the practice of repurposing materials to create new goods while preserving resources and lessening the adverse effects of production on the environment. Upcycling, on the other hand, goes beyond recycling by imaginatively reusing materials to give them a new life and increased value. This essay delves into the fundamental ideas, advantages, and difficulties surrounding recycling and upcycling, highlighting their critical roles in promoting a sustainable future.

One of the most essential tactics in the global drive to lessen the impact of garbage on the environment is recycling. The conventional "take-make-dispose" linear paradigm of production and consumption has led to the depletion of finite resources and the creation of enormous waste. Recycling puts materials back into the production cycle, upsetting this linear flow. Glass, plastics, metals, and paper are common recyclable materials. These resources go through several procedures to create new goods, including gathering, sorting, cleaning, and reprocessing. Recycling has several benefits, including preserving raw materials, using less energy than traditional production, using less landfill space, and reducing pollution from extracting and processing virgin materials.

Plastic recycling has gained popularity in light of the worrying problem of plastic pollution in seas and ecosystems. The whole plastics life cycle—from manufacture to disposal—significantly impacts the environment. By keeping plastic trash out of landfills and incinerators, recycling plastic helps lessen these effects. While chemical recycling converts plastic polymers back into their original monomers for future use, mechanical recycling entails melting and reforming plastic into new goods. However, there are obstacles to recycling plastics, such as the need for better infrastructure for collecting, the difficulty of separating different types of plastic, and the inability to recycle some plastics because of contamination or deterioration.

Upcycling provides a unique and inventive method of trash transformation beyond regular recycling. Upcycling is reusing waste materials to create new, frequently more valuable goods. It goes beyond simple material recovery. Upcycling maintains an item's original shape while improving its functionality or beauty; in contrast, recycling reduces things to their most basic forms. This process, which transforms what could be seen as garbage into valuable and distinctive inventions, calls for inventiveness and imagination. By prolonging the life of materials, lowering the need for new resources, and encouraging more mindful and sustainable consumption practices, upcycling helps reduce waste.

Designers, artists, and businesspeople have adopted upcycling to express creativity and solve environmental issues. Upcycling used fabrics or apparel into fashionable new items is known as upcycled fashion. By doing this, textile waste is decreased, and the ecologically harmful practices of the fast fashion business are contested. Through furniture upcycling, outdated or abandoned furniture parts are given new life and transformed into valuable and beautiful objects. A more sustainable and circular economy is promoted by upcycled items, which have a distinct appeal and provide customers with an alternative to mass-produced goods. These products are frequently handcrafted and customized.

Beyond only reducing trash, upcycling also has the potential to foster social innovation and economic development. Upcycling companies, frequently based in nearby areas, provide job and skill-development possibilities. Upcycling encourages a culture of inventive material reuse, which shifts consumer behavior toward more sustainable and conscientious purchases. The upcycling movement is greatly aided by regional craftspeople and small companies, who lessen the environmental effects of industrial production while reviving traditional skills and crafts.

But there are difficulties involved with upcycling. Because each upcycled product is generally one-of-a-kind and handcrafted, its scalability may be restricted. A delicate balance must be struck between achieving mass manufacturing and preserving the uniqueness and originality of recycled items. Consumer acceptance and knowledge also play a part; instead of following the rules of mass-produced commodities, upcycled items require a mental change to recognize their worth and narrative. Notwithstanding these obstacles, there appears to be a positive trend toward a more sustainable and circular economy, as seen by the rising demand for upcycled goods.

Moreover, recycling and upcycling are essential in solving the problem of electronic trash, or "e-waste." Because technology is developing so quickly, many electronic items are thrown away, polluting the environment and depleting vital resources. Recycling e-waste takes resources from abandoned electronic equipment, such as metals, polymers, and rare earth elements. The sustainable use of electronic components is encouraged by the proper disposal and recycling of e-waste, which also helps to avoid the release of harmful compounds into the environment. Furthermore, upcycling projects ingeniously reuse outdated electronics to create one-of- a-kind artwork, valuable gadgets, or instructional resources.

Supportive policies, public knowledge, and efficient waste management systems are necessary to succeed in recycling and upcycling projects. Thorough garbage collection and sorting procedures are required to guarantee that recyclables are appropriately handled and kept out of landfills. Campaigns for public education are essential in raising knowledge of the value of recycling, supporting appropriate disposal techniques, and highlighting the advantages of selecting upcycled goods. Through initiatives that encourage sustainable behaviors, such as extended producer responsibility (EPR) programs and financial incentives for companies using circular economy models, governments and corporations may also play a significant role in promoting recycling and upcycling.

Recycling and upcycling are not cure-alls, but they provide practical answers to trash-related problems. The cooperation of people, communities, corporations, and governments is essential to the success of these initiatives. The maxim "reduce, reuse, recycle" emphasizes how crucial it is to minimize trash output initially. A more sustainable approach to resource usage involves consuming less, choosing items with less packaging, and adopting a circular economy attitude.

Moreover, advances in product design and materials science are essential to achieving the objectives of upcycling and recycling. Encouraging recyclability and upgradability in product design helps with end-of-life procedures. The adverse effects of waste on the environment may be mitigated using sustainable packing materials and biodegradable alternatives. To promote the creation of goods that align with sustainability and circularity principles, innovation in material science and design must be driven by collaboration between industries, researchers, and designers.

Recycling and upcycling are revolutionary waste management techniques with significant effects on the planet's health and our ecological imprint. Addressing the environmental issues raised by growing trash requires transitioning from a linear economy to a circular economy, where resources are recycled and reused. While upcycling adds a creative and inventive element and transforms trash into valuable and distinctive crafts, recycling saves resources and lessens the environmental effect of production. Both strategies support a more sustainable and circular economy by encouraging social innovation, economic empowerment, and environmental stewardship. Embracing the principles of recycling and upcycling becomes a practical solution and a powerful expression of our collective commitment to a more sustainable and harmonious future as people, communities, and societies realize how urgent it is to address waste-related issues.

CHAPTER VII

Eco-Friendly Shelter

Sustainable Home Construction

The worldwide drive for sustainability has infiltrated all facets of our lives, including the manner in which we construct and occupy our houses. The concept of sustainable house construction has arisen as an important solution to environmental issues. This approach seeks to reduce the ecological effect of building methods and to produce homes that are in harmony with the natural world. This essay delves into the holistic approach that encompasses considerations such as material choices, resource conservation, and the overall ecological footprint of the built environment. It examines the principles, techniques, and benefits of sustainable home construction, delving into the holistic approach that goes beyond energy efficiency.

At the heart of sustainable house building is a dedication to minimizing the negative effects that the built environment has on the surrounding environment. This commitment takes into account not just the construction phase but also the operation of the home during its lifetime. Efficiency in energy use is an essential component, which includes the use of design techniques that maximize the use of natural light, ventilation, and thermal performance. A good example of passive solar architecture is the utilization of the sun's energy for heating purposes during the winter months, while shading structures during the summer months. This reduces the need for mechanical heating and cooling systems significantly. An additional factor that helps reduce the carbon footprint that is linked with the energy consumption of a home is the utilization of energy-efficient appliances, high-performance insulation, and renewable energy sources such as solar panels.

In environmentally responsible house building, the selection of materials is of the utmost importance. Construction methods that are considered traditional frequently make use of materials that are both resource-intensive and damaging to the environment, such as ordinary timber and concrete. Materials that have been recycled or recovered are examples of sustainable alternatives. These materials prevent trash from being dumped in landfills and lessen the demand for virgin resources. Engineered wood products, such as laminated veneer lumber (LVL) or cross-laminated timber (CLT), provide alternatives to conventional lumber that are more environmentally friendly. These materials give strength and durability while reducing their impact on the environment. An additional factor that helps to the sustainability of home building is the utilization of materials that are fast renewable, such as bamboo or cork. This is because these materials ensure a rapid regrowth cycle.

LEED, which stands for Leadership in Energy and Environmental Design, and BREEAM, which stands for Building Research Establishment Environmental Assessment Method, are examples of green building certification systems that offer frameworks for evaluating and encouraging sustainable construction practices. There are many other variables that are taken into consideration by these programs, such as the selection of the location, water efficiency, interior air quality, and innovative design. The attainment of certification through such programs is a demonstration of dedication to ecologically responsible building methods, which in turn encourages a more widespread adoption of sustainable building standards throughout the construction sector.

The conservation of water is an essential factor to take into consideration while building a sustainable home. A reduction in water use can be achieved by the implementation of water-saving plumbing fixtures, rainwater collection systems, and landscape designs that give priority to drought-resistant and native plant species. Greywater systems are an example of a sustainable approach to water management. These systems recycle water from activities such as bathing and washing for the purpose of using it for irrigation projects. Through the reduction of water use and the implementation of water recycling technologies that are both effective and efficient, sustainable homes make a contribution to the conservation of this valuable resource while also lowering the total environmental impact of the built environment.

By utilizing natural components, passive design concepts complement efforts to improve energy efficiency. This allows for the creation of a living environment that is both comfortable and environmentally friendly. It is possible to maximize the amount of natural light and ventilation in a home while simultaneously decreasing the amount of artificial heating or cooling that is required. This may be accomplished by strategically placing windows, orienting a home, and strategically using shading devices. Buildings that are environmentally responsible often have walls, roofs, and floors that are highly insulated to adjust the temperatures within the residence, hence eliminating the need for continuous mechanical climate control. A more harmonious relationship between the inhabitants and their surroundings is fostered as a result of the use of passive design methods, which not only improves energy efficiency but also serves to boost energy efficiency.

As a result of the significant influence that the building industry has on the development of trash and the utilization of landfills, waste minimization is an essential component of environmentally responsible home construction. Through the exact production of components off-site and the subsequent assembly of those components at the building site, prefabrication and modular construction processes help to reduce the amount of waste generated on. In addition, deconstruction procedures entail the meticulous disassembly of pre-existing buildings in order to rescue elements that may be reused. This helps to prevent these materials from being disposed of in landfills and contributes to a more circular and environmentally responsible building process. The ecological footprint of building projects may be further reduced by implementing construction waste management plans that encourage recycling and reuse. These plans are in line with the wider aims of sustainable construction.

The quality of the interior environment is frequently prioritized in sustainable houses because of the influence it has on the health and well-being of the people who live there. Maintaining a high level of indoor air quality requires the use of paints and finishes that contain low levels of volatile organic compounds (VOC), materials that do not contain formaldehyde, and ventilation systems that are adequate. The health-conscious design of sustainable houses is further enhanced by the use of natural and non-toxic building materials, such as clay plasters or recycled glass worktops. Not only do these factors help to the well-being of the inhabitants, but they also demonstrate a grasp of the connectivity that exists between the built environment and human health.

The construction of homes that consume no energy at all is an ambitious but attainable objective in the field of sustainable home building. Energy storage systems, energy-efficient architecture, and renewable energy sources are often utilized in conjunction with one another to achieve the goal of producing an equal amount of energy as they consume in these homes. Households that consume no energy at all are becoming more and more practical as a result of technological advancements such as solar panels that are extremely efficient and energy storage options such as home batteries. These houses are a prime example of the potential for sustainable building to not only lessen the negative impact on the environment but also actively contribute to the creation of a built environment that is both regenerative and carbon neutral. They do this by generating clean energy on-site and decreasing energy consumption through efficiently designed residences.

Not only can sustainable communities and eco-villages serve as examples of a comprehensive approach to sustainable living, but they also extend beyond individual dwellings. These intentional communities place an emphasis on environmentally responsible building techniques, renewable energy sources, and common areas that encourage a sense of connection and shared responsibility among their members. The goal of sustainable community design is to develop living environments that are resilient and regenerative, therefore reducing the negative impact on the environment while simultaneously improving the quality of life for people. This is accomplished by taking into consideration a wider range of elements, including transportation, food production, and waste management.

However, there are obstacles that must be overcome before sustainable house construction approaches may become generally used. Some homeowners and developers may be dissuaded from adopting sustainable building techniques due to the perceived complexity of these technologies, as well as economic concerns and initial expenses associated with implementation. On the other hand, the initial expenditure is frequently outweighed by the long-term advantages, which include decreased running expenses, higher property value, and savings on energy use respectively. The construction industry and homeowners can be encouraged to prioritize sustainability through the use of government incentives such as tax credits or subsidies for sustainable building projects. These types of incentives can play a key role in supporting sustainability.

When it comes to overcoming obstacles in the way of environmentally responsible house construction, education and awareness are essential components. By educating homeowners, builders, and architects on the advantages of sustainable practices, the technologies that are already accessible, and the impact that these practices will have on the environment over the long term, it is possible to encourage a more general awareness and acceptance of sustainable building approaches. Demonstrating successful case studies and displaying sustainable houses that are both visually beautiful and ecologically responsible are two ways to help dispel the perception that sustainability comes at the expense of design or comfort.

In coclusion, sustainable house construction is at the forefront of the worldwide trend toward living in a manner that is responsible to the environment. By incorporating energy-efficient design, sustainable materials, water conservation measures, and a comprehensive approach to waste reduction, sustainable houses are a prime example of a relationship that is both regenerative and harmonious between human habitation and the natural world. The development of environmentally friendly homes is becoming not only a choice but rather a responsibility as the general public becomes more aware of the critical nature of tackling climate change and the destruction of the environment. By embracing sustainable building practices, individuals, communities, and the construction industry can make a contribution to a future that is greener and more sustainable. This future will be one in which the places we call home embody the principles of environmental stewardship, resource conservation, and a commitment to building a better world for future generations.

Tiny Houses and Off-Grid Living

As a fascinating alternative way of life, tiny houses and off-grid living have gained hold in a society characterized by urbanization, consumerism, and environmental worries. A growing number of people are opting to reduce the size of their living areas and disengage from traditional grid-based services to embrace the principles of minimalism, sustainability, and self-sufficiency. This article goes into the philosophy behind tiny houses and off-grid living, examining the reasons for these lifestyle choices, the difficulties they provide, and their potential to bring about a transformational change in terms of creating a healthy connection with the environment and rethinking concepts of home.

To get to the heart of the matter, the tiny home movement is a movement that pushes for living areas that are simple and generally vary from 100 to 400 square feet. The prevalent belief that larger homes are associated with a more excellent quality of life is challenged by these tiny residences, emphasizing usefulness and efficiency. The design philosophy underpinning tiny houses emphasizes making creative use of space, possessing furniture that serves many purposes, and developing novel storage solutions to optimize usefulness while occupying a small footprint. Tiny houses are a trend that gained steam in the early 21st century, motivated by a desire for financial independence, environmental sustainability, and rejecting the excesses associated with mainstream housing. Although tiny houses have existed for some time, they are not new.

When people decide to live in tiny houses, one of the key reasons they do so is because they want to simplify their lifestyle and achieve financial independence. As a result of the high expense of conventional residences, as well as the weight of mortgages, property taxes, and energy costs, many people have needed to make decisions on their housing options. Because they are often less expensive to construct or buy, tiny homes achieve homeownership without the financial burden typically connected with more prominent buildings. Individuals can devote money to experiences, travel, education, and personal development because of the lower expenditures associated with tiny houses. This contrasts the situation in which they are tied to the financial commitment of maintaining a bigger home.

The concept of environmental sustainability is a fundamental principle that underpins the tiny home movement. This principle is in line with the overarching philosophy of reducing ecological footprints. Tiny houses are characterized by their small size, necessitating using fewer materials during the building process. This, in turn, reduces the demand for natural resources and minimizes waste associated with construction. The environmental sustainability of tiny houses is further improved by the fact that they emphasize energy efficiency, renewable energy sources, and living off the grid. Solar panels, composting toilets, and rainwater collection systems are some of the options that many people living in small houses choose to implement to lessen their dependency on conventional utilities and their environmental influence.

Off-grid living diverges from the traditional dependence on municipal services and centralized infrastructure, frequently combined with the tiny home lifestyle. Off-grid living entails generating power, managing water supplies, and processing trash disposal autonomously, often relying on different forms of renewable energy and environmentally responsible behaviors. A holistic approach to environmental responsibility and self-sufficiency arises from the synergy between off-grid and tiny home living styles. Individuals can handle issues such as power outages or water shortages more successfully when utilizing off-grid solutions because of their decentralized character, which builds resilience.

There are specific difficulties associated with the tiny home movement despite it promoting a less complicated and more ecologically responsible lifestyle. Several places have zoning restrictions and construction codes that potentially create issues for the lawful installation of tiny dwellings. Because many governments have minimum square footage housing restrictions, making tiny houses inside preexisting urban or suburban regions is challenging. Tiny homes are now being advocated for as a feasible and sustainable dwelling choice, and attempts are being made to solve the regulatory constraints preventing their widespread acceptance.

When individuals embrace tiny homes and off-grid living, it frequently includes a paradigm change in how they see and prioritize their living areas. Because of this, it is necessary to reassess one's assets, with the priority being placed on quality rather than quantity. As part of downsizing, individuals are required to tackle the consumerist mindset deeply embedded in contemporary society. This attitude challenges the concept that pleasure and fulfillment are related to acquiring material belongings. Adopting a minimalist lifestyle encourages individuals to place more importance on experiences, relationships, and personal well-being than on accumulating material goods.

The concepts of simplicity and utility are reflected in the design and architecture of tiny dwellings when constructed. It is essential to incorporate space-saving elements such as concealed storage compartments, folding furniture, and lofted sleeping quarters to maximize the available space. Many tiny houses have skylights and expansive windows to maximize the amount of natural light that enters the space and provide an open and airy environment. Various design aesthetics, ranging from rustic and traditional to modern and minimalist, frequently reflect the interests and values of the people who live in any given space.

The small home movement is not limited to a specific demographic but encompasses many people looking for alternatives to traditional ways of life. Tiny homes are seen as affordable for young adults who are frequently affected by a load of student loans and are confronted with economic instability to achieve property and financial independence. Tiny houses allow retirees and those with children no longer living at home to downsize, simplify their lives, and concentrate on experiences rather than the upkeep of a bigger home. Many tiny houses are located in rural or natural locations, which is another reason why the movement is appealing to those looking to have a more intimate relationship with the natural world.

Even though small houses are frequently linked with a nomadic or mobile way of life, some people prefer to build their tiny houses on wheels, while others decide to make them on more permanent foundations. A feeling of community may be fostered, resources can be shared, and a collective adoption of the concepts of minimalism and sustainability can be achieved by forming tiny house communities, which consist of clusters of compact residences. A collaborative approach to life is reflected in these intentional communities, which frequently include shared spaces, communal gardens, and cooperative efforts.

The revolutionary potential of small houses extends beyond the sphere of the individual and can affect more significant social trends and viewpoints on different housing solutions. As a result of the movement, cultural standards about homeownership are being reexamined, and the prevalent assumptions that correlate success with the size and grandeur of one's dwelling are being called into question. Tiny house proponents contend that the movement can contribute to resolving issues with the cost of housing, the density of urban areas, and the sustainability of the environment by encouraging the creative and effective utilization of available resources.

At the same time as people are becoming more conscious of the adverse effects of conventional housing practices on the environment, the small home movement is gaining popularity. In addition to contributing significantly to energy use, carbon emissions, and urban sprawl, the building and upkeep of large homes also contribute heavily. Small houses, on the other hand, offer a model for living that is more sustainable and environmentally friendly because they consume fewer resources and have designs that are more energy efficient. Conversations on responsible consumption, waste reduction, and the significance of leading a mindful and purposeful life are sparked as a result of the movement.

Using tiny dwellings as a canvas for experimenting with alternative building materials and environmentally responsible building procedures is another benefit of miniature homes. Some builders of small houses emphasize using ecologically friendly materials, such as recycled metals, repurposed wood, and non-toxic coatings. It is also possible to choose atypical settings for tiny houses because of their small size, providing greater flexibility. This flexibility can include reusing existing structures or merging with natural landscapes to minimize the environmental impact.

Regarding the obstacles connected with downsizing, critics of the tiny house movement express fair concerns. These challenges include restricted storage space, the possibility of discomfort, and the question of whether or not it is feasible to live in such small places for an extended period. Additionally, the regulatory difficulties associated with zoning and construction standards in many locations might hinder the general adoption of small homes as a mainstream dwelling alternative. To effectively address these difficulties, advocates of the movement, local governments, and regulatory agencies must engage in collaborative discourse, advocacy, and continuing collaboration.

In conclusion, the small house movement and off-grid living reflect a paradigm change in how individuals think about and experience their homes. These choices in lifestyle express a philosophy that places a high priority on sustainability, self-sufficiency, and deliberate living. This philosophy extends beyond the physical elements of downsizing and embracing minimalism. In terms of homeownership, consumerism, and the influence that housing choices have on the environment, the movement challenges the standards society has previously established. Individuals adopting tiny homes and off-grid living may contribute to a more significant societal change toward more sustainable and conscientious living. This shift may be motivated by financial reasons, environmental concerns, or a desire for a simpler and more meaningful existence. As the movement continues to develop, it provokes contemplation on the meaning of the term "home," the significance of connection, and the opportunities for creating a more harmonious relationship with the natural and the constructed surroundings.

CHAPTER VIII

Off-Grid Technology

Communication Solutions

Communication is the essence of human connection, and it significantly impacts our interpersonal relationships, civilizations, and the global community. The need for efficient communication solutions has never been more pressing than it is now, given the rapid advancement of technology and the world's growing interconnectedness. The complex landscape of communication solutions is investigated in this article. The study delves into the development of communication technologies, the problems and possibilities that these technologies bring, and the transformational influence that these technologies have on individuals, businesses, and society as a whole.

It is a monument to our fundamental urge to connect and exchange information that the history of human communication illustrates. Beginning with the creation of cave art and oral traditions and the development of written language and the printing press, each new technical advancement has increased the scope of human communication and the effectiveness of its delivery. As a result of the introduction of telegraphy, the telephone, and the internet, the modern period has witnessed a revolution in how we communicate. This change has resulted in the elimination of geographical borders and the establishment of a global village.

The growth of digital communication technology is one of the most significant transformational events that has occurred in the most recent decades. The internet originated from research conducted by the military and students at academic institutions and has developed into a pervasive force in almost every facet of our lives. In recent years, electronic mail, instant messaging, social networking, and video conferencing have emerged as indispensable personal and professional communication tools. The widespread availability of smartphones and high-speed internet access has brought about further acceleration of communication. This has enabled people worldwide to engage in real-time and share information.

The landscape of interpersonal communication has been significantly altered due to the proliferation of social media platforms. Through these platforms, users are granted access to information, news, and the personal lives of others previously unattainable. They function as online communities where individuals can converse about their thoughts, experiences, and opinions, establishing connections and difficulties. Influencing public opinion and activism and even creating political landscapes, the immediacy and accessibility of social media have enhanced the effect of information dissemination, which has led to an increase in the impact of information dissemination.

Even though digital communication technologies have many advantages, they also present several obstacles. These issues include concerns over privacy, an abundance of information, and disseminating false information. The quick broadcast of data, which frequently occurs without the inclusion of appropriate verification, might contribute to the growth of false news and the destruction of faith in conventional media sources. The algorithmic curating of material on social media platforms might lead to the formation of echo chambers, the reinforcement of preexisting opinions, and the restriction of exposure to various perspectives.

Within the context of the digital era, privacy has emerged as a primary concern. Regarding consent, transparency, and the potential for misusing information, the acquisition, storage, and analysis of personal data by technology corporations raises ethical problems. The necessity for rigorous measures to protect digital communication channels is highlighted by the fact that cybersecurity threats, ranging from data breaches to identity theft, are becoming increasingly prevalent. The difficulty of finding a middle ground between the ease of use of digital communication and the safeguarding of personal privacy continues to be faced by those who create technology and formulate public policy.

Innovations such as 5G networks and the Internet of Things (IoT) have been brought about due to the desire for a smooth and secure connection. The ongoing development of communication technology has brought about this demand. A new age of connection will be enabled by 5G, which promises to bring quicker and more reliable wireless communication. This revolution will have consequences for various industries, including healthcare and transportation. This offers potential for smart homes, communities, and businesses but raises questions about data security, interoperability, and the ethical implications of a hyper-connected society. The Internet of Things (IoT) connects everyday items to the internet.

Communication solutions are critical in business since they play a crucial role in increasing efficiency, cooperation, and innovation. As a result of global events such as the COVID-19 pandemic, remote work trends have become more prevalent, bringing to light the significance of having a reliable communication infrastructure. Platforms for video conferencing, project management tools, and collaborative work software have transformed into indispensable resources for teams dispersed across many geographic locations. The move toward working from home has changed the dynamics of conventional offices and caused businesses to reevaluate their communication techniques to encourage employee engagement and ensure that they continue to feel a sense of community among their workforce.

When it comes to communication solutions, incorporating artificial intelligence (AI) and machine learning (ML) brings about both new opportunities and new obstacles. Virtual assistants and chatbots that are driven by artificial intelligence improve customer service and expedite conversations. Natural language processing makes Voice-activated communication possible, making devices such as smart speakers and virtual assistants more user-friendly and intuitive. However, there are ethical concerns that surround artificial intelligence, such as the possibility of job displacement and the existence of prejudice in algorithms. These concerns call for thorough analysis and regulation.

Patient care, diagnosis, and treatment are all areas in which the implementation of communication technologies in the healthcare industry might significantly improve. Telemedicine, made possible by developments in technology such as video conferencing and remote monitoring, gives patients the ability to get medical consultations without having to leave the convenience of their homes. The data acquired about a person's health via mobile applications and wearable devices provides patients and healthcare practitioners with valuable additional insights. However, to achieve widespread acceptance of telemedicine, it is necessary to overcome difficulties with protecting personal information, legal frameworks, and equal access to technology.
A shift has also occurred in the education field due to the advent of the digital era. Communication technologies have become an essential component of online education and remote learning. Educational applications, collaboration platforms, and virtual classrooms all work

together to improve access to information and make engaging students in interactive learning experiences easier. On the other hand, the digital gap, characterized by differences in internet access and technology resources, presents obstacles to ensuring that all individuals have equal access to educational opportunities.

Emerging technologies that push the boundaries of what is now achievable are expected to impact the future of communication solutions significantly. The concepts of augmented reality (AR) and virtual reality (VR) have the potential to produce completely immersive communication experiences. These experiences range from interactive instructional simulations to virtual meetings. There are uses for blockchain technology that can improve the security and transparency of communication channels. Blockchain technology is most recognized for its role in creating a secure environment for transactions. Because it is based on the laws of quantum physics, quantum communication can provide an unprecedented level of security when it comes to transmitting sensitive information.

Ethical issues are becoming more critical as the technology that facilitates communication continues to evolve. To ensure the development and deployment of these technologies in a responsible manner, it is necessary to have a complete awareness of their possible impact on society. Issues such as digital inclusion, privacy rights, data ownership, and the ethical use of artificial intelligence require deliberate and transparent methods from those who build technology, those who determine legislation, and society as a whole all at the same time.
In conclusion, communication solutions have progressed beyond the straightforward transmission of information to the development of intricate, linked systems that define the landscapes of our personal lives, professional lives,

and lives in society. Although it enables seamless worldwide communication, the high rate of technological innovation also raises worries about privacy and the ethical implications of artificial intelligence. The rapid speed of technical advancement brings about these benefits and problems. A multidisciplinary strategy that considers technological innovation, ethical issues, and a commitment to inclusion is required to navigate this complicated landscape successfully. It will be vital to discover solutions that strike a balance between the progression of technology and the ethical duty to construct a connected, informed, and equal future. Communication will continue to be a driving force in human progress.

DIY Electronics

Individuals have been given the ability to tinker, experiment, and create thanks to the do-it-yourself (DIY) philosophy, which has emerged as a driving force behind many breakthroughs throughout history. The spirit of do-it-yourself (DIY) has taken on new dimensions in the field of electronics, making it possible for enthusiasts, amateurs, and innovators to investigate the complexities of circuits, components, and programming. This article delves into the realm of do-it-yourself electronics, tracing its origins, analyzing its development, and underlining its influence on education, innovation, and the democratization of technology.

DIY electronics may be traced back to the early days of radio and electronics hobbyist groups in the early 20th century. These communities were active during the early years of the century. At the same time as radio transmission was capturing the general public's interest, individuals anxious to investigate the potential of wireless communication started experimenting with creating their own radios and other electronic equipment. Magazines such as "Popular Mechanics" and "Radio Electronics" were essential in the development of the do-it-yourself (DIY) movement because they offered hobbyists circuit diagrams, instructions, and a sense of community.

As leftover military technology became available to the general population in the years following World War II, there was a meteoric rise in the number of people interested in electronics. In conjunction with the increasing availability of inexpensive vacuum tubes and transistors, the proliferation of components has produced an atmosphere ideal for do-it-yourself experimentation. The proliferation of electronic hobbyist groups and amateur radio operators helped to cultivate a culture that values the exchange of information and the working together of peers. Many people have found that do-it-yourself electronics have become a portal to understanding the inner workings of technology and engaging in hands-on learning.

Simply put, introducing the personal computer in the 1970s was a watershed event for do-it-yourself electronics. Because of the proliferation of open-source hardware and software and the availability of microprocessors at reasonable prices, a new wave of experimentation has been made possible. Homebrew computer clubs, which were gathering places for enthusiasts to exchange ideas and display their do-it-yourself computers, were an essential component in the development of the personal computing revolution. The do-it-yourself (DIY) philosophy emphasizing the potential of individual invention and innovation inspired the famous Apple I, which Steve Wozniak and Steve Jobs created. Do-it-yourself electronics have been at the vanguard of this movement, leading to the democratization of technology in the 21st century. An entirely new generation of makers has been allowed to explore the realms of electronics and programming due to the availability of low-cost microcontrollers like Arduino and Raspberry Pi. These platforms offer readily available entry points for novices, enabling users to construct and experiment with various projects, ranging from straightforward LED displays to complex Internet of Things (IoT) devices.

The ethos of do-it-yourself electronics is encapsulated in the maker movement, which took off in the early 2000s and acquired massive momentum. Individuals can pursue their electronic and engineering projects in a collaborative setting that is supplied with tools and materials. Makerspaces have become centers for individuals to explore their ideas. Makers can bring their electronic dreams to life with the help of Arduino, which has become a symbol of the maker movement because of its user-friendly interface and enormous community support. Do-it-yourself electronics have had a significant influence on the educational system. Hands-on electronics projects are increasingly included in traditional STEM (science, technology, engineering, and mathematics) instruction to engage students and promote a better grasp of STEM ideas. Learning about physics, mathematics, and programming may be done in a way that is both physical and engaging through the use of do-it-yourself electronics. Students of any age can receive an education in electronics via educational kits and platforms like the BBC Micro bit and Adafruit Circuit Playground. These kits and platforms provide a structured but hands-on approach to teaching students about electronics.

In addition, do-it-yourself electronics are significant in closing the gender gap in STEM disciplines. Individuals of all genders are allowed to participate in hands-on experimentation and creativity through the field of do-it-yourself electronics, which provides learning environments that are inclusive and collaborative. To motivate the future generation of diverse technologists and engineers, initiatives such as "Girls Who Code" and organizations that promote STEM education for underrepresented populations use the accessibility of do-it-yourself electronics.

Do-it-yourself electronics are characterized by several qualities, one of which is the focus on open-source hardware and software. Collaboration, the sharing of information, and the unrestricted interchange of ideas are all encouraged by the open-source philosophy. For do-it-yourself (DIY) electronics hobbyists, platforms like GitHub have become significant centers where they can share their creations, source code, and documentation. This culture of collaboration has resulted in the establishment of a massive ecosystem consisting of libraries, tutorials, and resources, which has resulted in creating a community that is very supportive of both novice and expert makers.

The realm of do-it-yourself electronics construction comprises diverse tasks, ranging from straightforward and functional to intricate and cutting-edge. Home improvement enthusiasts have constructed various electronic art pieces and home automation systems, including robotic devices, synthesizers, and other electronic equipment. This yearly event, known as the Maker Faire, celebrates creativity, ingenuity, and resourcefulness. It highlights the diversity and inventiveness within the community of do-it-yourself electronics enthusiasts. Interdisciplinary projects that push the frontiers of what is possible have been produced due to the interaction of electronics with other fields of study, such as art, design, and music.

Because it is both open-source and modular, Arduino has become an indispensable component in do-it-yourself electrical projects. Because of its adaptability and user-friendliness, it is a perfect platform for working with various applications. Arduino has evolved into a platform allowing creators to express their creativity in multiple ways, including creating interactive installations and wearable electronics and constructing bespoke instruments and appliances for the smart home. Many sensors, actuators, and shields are included in the thriving ecosystem surrounding Arduino. These components enhance the possibilities of the Arduino platform, allowing creators to experiment with various devices and projects.

Raspberry Pi is another prominent platform in the realm of do-it-yourself electronics. Its primary objective is to provide educational institutions with a computer that is credit card tiny and inexpensive. Raspberry Pi has been utilized in various applications, including robots, media centers, vintage gaming consoles, and even do-it-yourself home servers. The fact that it is both easily accessible and reasonably priced has helped to its broad acceptance, making it an excellent alternative for projects that need a computing platform that is both tiny and exceptionally powerful.

Over and beyond the domain of hobbyist projects, the influence of do-it-yourself electronics extends into the realm of business and innovation. The community of do-it-yourself electronics enthusiasts is the origin of many successful enterprises. Crowdfunding sites such as Kickstarter and Indiegogo have provided do-it-yourself innovators with a platform from which they may bring their ideas to market. A mindset driven by creativity, iteration, and fast prototyping has been created due to the Maker Movement. These are characteristics that are essential to the success of an entrepreneur.

The rise of low-cost 3D printing technology has significantly expanded the do-it-yourself movement. Constructors can now prototype and construct individualized enclosures, components, and even whole devices with reasonable simplicity. Individuals can now transform their ideas into concrete items without needing large-scale production facilities because of the democratization of manufacturing methods.

That said, the world of do-it-yourself electronics is full of difficulties. The availability of resources, tools, and mentoring continues to be a pressing matter, particularly in economically disadvantaged areas. It is necessary to make significant efforts in education, outreach, and community building to bridge the digital gap and ensure that chances for do-it-yourself electronics are accessible to various people.

In addition, the quick rate of technical progress might function as a barrier for individuals who are new to the field. People who are just beginning may find the enormous diversity of components, programming languages, and platforms intimidating. To lower entrance barriers and make do-it-yourself electronics more accessible to a broader audience, it is vital to have effective onboarding tactics, instructional materials, and mentorship programs.

Exciting discoveries are on the horizon within the community of do-it-yourself electronics enthusiasts, which is constantly evolving. The incorporation of artificial intelligence and machine learning into do-it-yourself projects results in the creation of new opportunities for intelligent systems and smart gadgets. With the increasing availability of edge computing, developers can construct apps that require low latency and real-time responsiveness. Edge computing is a type of computing in which data processing occurs on the device rather than in the cloud.

A developing trend is the convergence of do-it-yourself electronics with sustainable and suitable environmental activities. Those interested in making things are investigating initiatives that encourage waste reduction, energy efficiency, and environmental conservation. With projects ranging from solar-powered devices to recycling programs for electronic garbage, do-it-yourself electronics fans are actively contributing to a more environmentally friendly and socially responsible future in technology.

In conclusion, do-it-yourself electronics encompass the spirit of creativity, curiosity, and invention that motivates individuals to explore the world of electronics and do so on their terms. Throughout the history of technology, the do-it-yourself (DIY) philosophy has been crucial in influencing the landscape of the field, from the early days of radio hobbyists to the modern maker movement. As do-it-yourself electronics continue to develop, they provide a doorway for learning, a platform for invention, and a community that celebrates the joy of producing things. Do-it-yourself electronics allow people to be creators, innovators, and builders of their technological destiny. This helps to cultivate a culture of continual learning and hands-on exploration in the digital era. Some examples of DIY electronics include the construction of a basic LED project and the design of a complicated Internet of Things gadget.

CHAPTER IX

Emergency Preparedness

Off-Grid First Aid

Whether in the vast landscapes of the wilderness, the remote regions of rural areas, or the unexplored territory of off-grid life, the requirement for first aid takes on a particular personality. "off-grid first aid" refers to a collection of abilities, information, and resources designed to meet health difficulties in settings where traditional medical support may be restricted or absent. This essay delves into the complexities of off-grid first aid, analyzing the specific factors to consider, the fundamental abilities necessary, and the significant techniques required to handle health emergencies in environments disconnected from the conventional healthcare infrastructure.

Recognizing the Obstacles Faced by Off-Grid Systems

Off-grid situations, distinguished by their isolation and absence of traditional conveniences, present a unique set of obstacles when it comes to providing medical aid. Individuals in these environments frequently experience longer response times for professional medical assistance. This is true whether they participate in an outdoor activity, live on a rural homestead, or live in an intended off-grid community. When dealing with health problems, it is essential to be self-sufficient because of the limited availability of resources, the unpredictability of environmental circumstances, and the lack of rapid access to medical services.

Essential Abilities for First Aid in Off-Grid Situations

Providing first aid in an off-grid environment requires a set of abilities that go beyond what is covered in standard first aid classes. It is imperative that those who are considering off-grid settings acquire the following critical skills: a top priority.

In wilderness first aid training, the primary focus is on responding to medical situations in isolated areas. It addresses evaluating injuries, treating wounds, and managing environmental variables such as exposure to high temperatures or problems connected to altitude. Given the restricted availability of medical resources in off-grid locations, WFA emphasizes the capacity to demonstrate creativity and adaptability.

Not only does off-grid first aid entail the treatment of injuries, but it also requires the ability to navigate challenging environments and communicate effectively. If assistance is needed, it is essential to possess fundamental navigational skills, including the ability to use maps and compasses and knowledge of various communication equipment, such as satellite phones and emergency beacons.

First aid and survival are sometimes difficult to discern in off-grid settings. An all-encompassing strategy for off-grid health should include the acquisition of skills such as the construction of shelter, the discovery of drinkable water, and the procurement of food. It is of the utmost importance to adjust to one's surroundings and maintain one's survival until either expert assistance arrives or the circumstances improve.

The lack of regular medical equipment may necessitate creativity while providing first aid in off-grid situations. For example, learning how to make splints out of readily available materials, fashioning bandages out of clothes, or using natural components for wound treatment are all improvised medical practices that are helpful in remote areas.

First-Aid Kits for Off-Grid Medical Supplies and Equipment

As a result of the specific difficulties that are presented by distant situations, the contents of an off-grid first aid kit are different from those utilized in conventional kits. Although individual requirements may differ depending on the specifics of the situation, a thorough off-grid first aid pack will generally consist of the following: When it comes to treating wounds caused by cuts, abrasions, or punctures, items such as sterile dressings, sticky bandages, antiseptic wipes, and medical tape are essential.

The severity of injuries that might occur in off-grid circumstances can range from not serious to severe. When handling major injuries until professional assistance is available, having items such as trauma shears, a tourniquet, and a pressure dressing readily available may be helpful.

It is essential to include any prescription prescriptions, primary pain relievers, antihistamines, and any other medications that individuals in the group may require. Keeping track of the expiration dates and the possible adverse effects is of the utmost importance.

Removing splinters and cutting fabric for makeshift bandages are just two examples of the many scenarios in which tweezers, scissors, and a multifunctional tool can prove invaluable.

An essential component of the first aid kit should include maps, compasses, and GPS devices. This is especially important in wilderness or isolated areas, where accurate navigation is necessary to locate assistance.

It is recommended that, in addition to a fully charged mobile phone, you also bring a satellite phone, an emergency beacon, or a two-way radio to ensure reliable connection in regions with limited cell service.

Access to clean water may need to be clarified when there is no grid connection. To prevent illnesses that are transmitted by water, it is vital to have water purification pills, a portable water filter, or other choices for water conditioning.

In many off-grid locations, hypothermia and exposure are potential dangers that might occur. In an emergency, emergency blankets, a small shelter, or a waterproof tarp can provide protection from the elements.

Not only does the ability to build a fire give warmth, but it also serves as a signal for rescue authorities to come and help. In addition to a good torch or headlamp with additional batteries, you should also have lighter or waterproof matches.

A watertight container should store pertinent health documents, critical medical information, and emergency contact information. This information is vital if healthcare workers require assistance from other sources.

Off-Grid First Aid Methods and Procedures

A systematic and methodical strategy is required to navigate health emergencies while off the grid. To correctly manage medical issues in distant areas, individuals might benefit from considering the following measures:

Conduct a comprehensive risk assessment before heading into locations not connected to the grid. Learn about the possible health risks associated with the environment, such as the local fauna, the weather patterns, and the obstacles posed by the geography. Your first aid preparations should be tailored to the threats that have been identified.

Not only does off-grid first aid include reacting to catastrophes, but it also involves preventing them from occurring. A significant reduction in the chance of accidents or health problems can be achieved with adequate preparation, including appropriate gear, clothes, and an understanding of the surrounding environment.

It is essential to devise a complete emergency plan that includes protocols for communication, designated meeting sites, and evacuation procedures. Take measures to ensure that every group member is aware of the plan and their responsibilities in the event of an emergency crisis.

Consider conducting first aid training sessions for all members of an off-grid community or group you are a part of. To a greater extent, the collective capacity to respond to emergencies is improved when more persons are prepared with fundamental first aid abilities.

Maintain awareness of the most recent advancements in first aid and wilderness medicine. You should maintain your skills by taking refresher classes, participating in seminars, and attending workshops. If you have more information, you can respond to health concerns associated with living off the grid with greater self-assurance and efficiency.

The ecology of an off-grid location is both dynamic and unexpected. Responding to unforeseen circumstances requires high adaptability and an openness to improvisation. Acquire the ability to make the most of the available resources and to think creatively when administering first aid.

It is essential to have a dependable method of contact with the outside world. When asking for expert assistance or providing updates, technologies such as satellite phones, emergency beacons, or two-way radios may be helpful.

Get familiar with the specific environmental elements in the off-grid site. Your capacity to predict and respond to potential health difficulties is improved when you are aware of your environment. This is true whether you are exposed to high altitudes, harsh temperatures, or specific species populations.

Gain a comprehensive grasp of how to handle emergencies. In a crisis, whether it be a catastrophic injury, an aggravation of a medical condition, or a natural catastrophe, a crisis management plan provides a more structured and successful response.

In addition to addressing the physical ailments that group members may be experiencing, off-grid first aid also considers the psychological well-being of those persons. One of the most critical aspects of off-grid health management is being sensitive to the psychological effects of events and offering help to those affected.

To be successful in the field of off-grid first aid, one must possess a distinct set of skills, be inventive, and be able to adapt to changing circumstances. The need to become self-sufficient in a health emergency is becoming increasingly apparent as many people adopt off-grid living, engage in outdoor activities, or establish intentional communities in isolated areas. Folks must proactively prepare for the outdoors by acquiring wilderness first aid training and putting together thorough off-grid first aid kits.

Evacuation Plans and Survival Skills

It is impossible to stress the significance of developing effective evacuation plans and polishing survival skills in a society characterized by natural catastrophes, emergencies, and unexpected crises that are difficult to forecast. To successfully traverse the way to safety, individuals and communities need to be well-prepared, regardless of whether they are confronted with the fury of hurricanes, wildfires, or unanticipated urban catastrophes. This article aims to dig into the complexities of evacuation planning and survival skills, examining the fundamental components, the role of community resilience, and the necessity of proactive actions to guarantee that individuals can successfully respond to and endure emergency circumstances.

Strategy for ensuring safety

Evacuation plans serve as the most critical component of disaster preparedness. They offer an organized and structured method, allowing for the rapid movement of persons away from imminent danger and into safety. These plans include a broad spectrum of emergencies, including natural catastrophes such as earthquakes and floods, as well as occurrences caused by humans, such as industrial mishaps or threats from terrorist organizations. Straightforward communication tactics, defined evacuation routes, assembly places, and contingency plans for persons with special needs are all essential to efficient evacuation preparations.

The participation and knowledge of the community is an essential component of the evacuation preparation process. The education of the general people about potential dangers and the actions to take during an evacuation is a crucial responsibility that falls on the shoulders of local governments, emergency services, and community groups. To cultivate a feeling of responsibility and preparation among communities, public awareness campaigns, exercises, and distribution of instructional materials all contribute to developing a well-informed citizenry.

An exhaustive risk assessment is required to design evacuation plans. This evaluation must consider the geographical and environmental elements affecting the targeted location. Planners can customize evacuation routes, identify safe zones, and efficiently distribute resources when they thoroughly understand the community's risks and strengths. Using technology, such as alarm systems and mapping tools, improves the effectiveness of evacuation plans by delivering information and direction in real-time during times of emergency.

In addition, evacuation preparations require a distinct chain of command and consistent coordination across the many different entities involved in disaster response. Local authorities, law enforcement, fire departments, and medical staff must cooperate to guarantee a smooth and well-organized evacuation procedure. Refinement of evacuation processes, identification of possible bottlenecks, and general improvement of response efforts are all benefits that may be achieved through regular training exercises and simulations.

The requirements of vulnerable groups, such as older people, those with impairments, and people with restricted mobility, should also be considered while developing evacuation plans. Community outreach initiatives, accessible shelters, and specialized transportation are all essential elements that should be included in an evacuation strategy that can accommodate everyone. It is possible to ensure that no one is left behind during emergency evacuations by tailoring strategies to fit the specific requirements of various communities.

Confronting and Overcoming Obstacles Developing survival skills empowers individuals to adapt and respond effectively in the face of hardship. At the same time, evacuation plans give an organized framework for relocating to a safe location. A vast number of talents are included in the category of survival skills. These skills can provide basic first aid and navigation, resourcefulness, resilience, and the capacity to make educated decisions under duress.

Knowing first aid is one of the most essential survival skills in an emergency since it enables individuals to offer rapid treatment to others who have been harmed. Fundamental training in first aid covers cardiopulmonary resuscitation (CPR), wound treatment, and the capacity to respond to standard medical crises. Individuals who are equipped with first aid skills have the potential to make a substantial impact in the preservation of life and the reduction of the severity of injuries in circumstances when professional medical assistance may be temporarily delayed.

It is essential for anyone who may find themselves in unfamiliar territory during an evacuation to have the ability to navigate. Your ability to navigate securely and arrive at specified assembly locations or shelters is improved when you know how to utilize current navigation instruments like maps, compasses, and other navigational aids. In addition, persons displaced for lengthy periods would benefit tremendously from understanding fundamental outdoor skills such as constructing shelters, locating sources of drinkable water, and making fires.

Another essential survival skill is communicating effectively, mainly when conventional communication routes are blocked. People can maintain touch with other people, coordinate their activities, and obtain vital information when they acquire the skills necessary to operate various communication equipment such as radios, signaling devices, and other communication tools. To improve the overall efficiency of reaction and evacuation activities, it is essential to have the capacity to communicate messages.

Within survival circumstances, adaptability and inventiveness are of the utmost importance. Individuals can manage unanticipated problems and make the most of limited resources if they are prepared with problem-solving skills and the capacity to provide improvised solutions. Examples of talents in this category include the ability to forage for food, purify water, and create improvised tools to meet urgent requirements. Resilience in the face of hardship is enhanced when one can think creatively and adjust to changing circumstances.

Maintaining one's emotional and psychological stability is an essential component of survival abilities that is frequently neglected. Individuals must acquire coping methods to handle stress, worry, and uncertainty when confronted with crises and evacuations, which can be emotionally exhausting. Through the cultivation of a mentality of resilience, the maintenance of attention in high-pressure situations, and the support of one's mental well-being as well as the mental well-being of others during and after catastrophes, mental readiness may be achieved.

Community resilience is an extension of individual survival skills that emphasizes the collective capacity of communities to resist, respond to, and recover from calamities. The overall resilience of a community may be improved by factors such as the establishment of mutual assistance networks, the development of strong social networks, and the promotion of cohesive communities. The capacity of a community to weather crises and assist one another during the evacuation and recovery phases is enhanced when resources, communication channels, and collaborative efforts are shared among community members.

A Plea for Intervening

In a society where the number of catastrophes and their severity is increasing, it is not only a good idea but a must to take preventative actions to improve one's survival ability in an emergency. Identifying risks, strengthening response capacities, and instilling a culture of readiness are all tasks that need collaboration between governments, communities, and individuals. The proactive approach to emergency preparedness includes several essential components, including public awareness campaigns, educational activities, and training programs.

The establishment and execution of comprehensive emergency management frameworks are essential responsibilities that fall under the purview of governments. Investing in public awareness campaigns, allocating resources for the formulation and regular updating of evacuation plans, and performing regular drills and exercises all contribute to establishing a robust disaster preparation infrastructure. Further enhancement of overall resilience may be achieved by implementing legislation and policies that prioritize the incorporation of evacuation plans into urban development, zoning rules, and public infrastructure projects.

Community participation is an essential component of constructing a proactive culture of readiness. Public education campaigns that teach citizens about potential threats, evacuation routes, and the significance of individual and communal preparedness should be a priority. Local authorities should prioritize these activities in partnership with community groups. Training programs, workshops, and simulation exercises in the community provide people with chances for hands-on learning and instill a feeling of responsibility.

Because individuals are the ultimate recipients of proactive preparedness measures, they are obligated to invest in their own readiness. Individuals can adopt preventative measures such as acquiring fundamental survival skills, training for first aid and emergency response, and maintaining awareness of local threats and evacuation protocols. Developing individual and familial resilience may be accomplished via activities such as putting together emergency supply kits, developing family emergency plans, and participating in community drills.

The utilization of technology in an efficient manner has the potential to improve proactive preparedness activities dramatically. Mobile applications, alert systems, and social media platforms are utilized to provide real-time information and communication channels during times of emergency. It is possible to guarantee that persons have access to vital information and resources by incorporating technology into evacuation plans and survival skill training. This is the case even when traditional means of communication may need to be improved.

To summarize, a complete strategy for disaster preparedness is formed by the combination of well-developed evacuation plans and the development of survival abilities that have been polished over time. As the world continues to see an increase in natural catastrophes, climate-related occurrences, and unanticipated crises, the necessity of taking preventative actions is becoming increasingly apparent. Survival skills equip individuals with the ability to adapt to and handle the hurdles presented by emergency circumstances. At the same time, evacuation plans serve as the blueprint for implementing coordinated responses. Individuals and communities may not only survive the storm but emerge more robust, more resilient, and better able to confront an uncertain future if they embrace a culture of preparedness and make it a part of their culture.

CHAPTER X

Celebrating Off-Grid Success Stories

Showcasing Successful Off-Grid Projects

In off-grid living, success stories serve as beacons of inspiration, demonstrating the tangible possibilities and the transformative power of sustainable, self-sufficient lifestyles. The chapter "Showcasing Successful Off-Grid Projects" aims to illuminate a spectrum of endeavors that have not only embraced the ethos of off-grid living but have also thrived in doing so. These projects, diverse in scope and scale, provide a glimpse into the innovative solutions, resilient structures, and sustainable practices that can be employed to create thriving off-grid oases.

One exemplary off-grid project revolves around an eco-friendly shelter designed with sustainability at its core. Utilizing recycled materials and employing passive solar design principles, this project showcases how a dwelling can harmonize with its natural surroundings while minimizing its environmental footprint. The success of such architectural endeavors lies not only in constructing a physical shelter but in creating a living space that embodies principles of self-sufficiency, energy efficiency, and a deep connection to the natural environment.

In energy independence, success stories abound with DIY solar power installations that have not only met but exceeded the energy needs of off-grid dwellers. These projects often involve a meticulous understanding of energy consumption patterns, efficient use of solar panels, and the implementation of advanced battery storage solutions. By showcasing these successes, the chapter aims to empower readers to embark on their solar power journeys, harnessing the inexhaustible power of the sun to sustain their off-grid lifestyles.

A thriving off-grid oasis is complete with a sustainable food production system, and success stories in this domain spotlight innovative gardening practices, vertical farming solutions, and aquaponic systems. These projects underscore the adaptability of off-grid cultivators to diverse climates and terrains, showcasing the possibilities of growing food in limited spaces with minimal environmental impact. The chapter delves into these success stories to inspire readers to cultivate their food, fostering a more profound sense of self-reliance and reducing dependence on external food sources.

Water, a fundamental resource for off-grid living, takes center stage in successful rainwater harvesting projects. Off-grid enthusiasts have ingeniously designed and implemented rainwater collection systems that efficiently capture, store and purify rainwater for various household needs. These projects emphasize the importance of water conservation, a key pillar of sustainable living, and serve as blueprints for individuals seeking to emulate these self-sustaining water solutions.

Transportation, often challenging in remote off-grid locations, witnesses success stories featuring DIY electric bikes, vehicles, and alternative eco-friendly transport modes. These initiatives showcase how off-grinders can reduce their carbon footprint while maintaining mobility, contributing to a more sustainable and interconnected lifestyle. By highlighting these inventive solutions, the chapter encourages readers to explore alternative transportation options that align with their off-grid ethos.

Success stories in off-grid living also extend to waste management and composting initiatives. Through innovative composting toilets, recycling systems, and zero-waste practices, off-grinders have minimized their environmental impact and created closed-loop systems where waste becomes a valuable resource. These projects highlight the transformative potential of adopting responsible waste management practices, reinforcing the principle of leaving minimal footprints on the environment.

The chapter further explores successful off-grid communication solutions, showcasing projects that have overcome limited connectivity challenges in remote locations. These initiatives leverage satellite technology, low-power communication devices, and community networks to establish reliable communication channels. By featuring these success stories, the chapter emphasizes the importance of staying connected locally and globally while navigating the demands of an off-grid lifestyle.

Additionally, the section on successful off-grid projects recognizes the importance of community building. Off grid communities have flourished through collaborative efforts, shared resources, and a collective commitment to sustainable living. These success stories demonstrate that the pursuit of off-grid independence does not equate to isolation but instead fosters a sense of belonging, mutual support, and a shared vision for a more sustainable future.

In conclusion, the chapter "Showcasing Successful Off-Grid Projects" is a testament to the diverse, innovative, and thriving off-grid projects that individuals and communities have undertaken. These success stories illuminate the transformative potential of sustainable, self-sufficient living, providing valuable insights and inspiration for those embarking on their off-grid journeys. Through a tapestry of accomplishments in eco-friendly shelter construction, energy independence, food production, water management, transportation, waste reduction, and community building, the chapter paints a vivid picture of the possibilities that await those who embrace the off-grid lifestyle with creativity, determination, and a commitment to sustainable living.

Learning from Real-Life Experiences

The chapter on "Learning from Real-Life Experiences" bridges theory and practice, providing readers with a rich tapestry of narratives and insights drawn from the actual experiences of individuals who have embarked on the challenging yet rewarding journey of off-grid living. These real-life stories offer a nuanced understanding of the triumphs, trials, and transformative moments that define the off-grid lifestyle, allowing readers to glean practical wisdom from those who have navigated the path before them.

Embedded within these narratives are lessons on the importance of adaptability in the face of ever-changing circumstances. Real-life off-grinders often deal with unforeseen challenges, be it extreme weather conditions, unexpected equipment failures, or the complexities of managing off-grid systems. Through their experiences, readers learn the value of resilience and the ability to adapt strategies, technologies, and lifestyles to suit the dynamic nature of off-grid living. These stories underscore that flexibility is a cornerstone of sustainable, off-grid success.

Furthermore, the section delves into the emotional and psychological aspects of off-grid living through the lens of real-life experiences. It candidly explores the highs and lows, the moments of solitude, and the communal joys that individuals and families encounter. These narratives serve as a compass for emotional preparedness, offering readers a glimpse into the mental fortitude required to navigate the potential isolation of remote living while highlighting the profound connection to nature and community that often accompanies an off-grid lifestyle.

Learning from real-life experiences also entails understanding the intricacies of sustainable food production. The chapter unveils narratives of individuals cultivating their food and facing the challenges of weather fluctuations, pests, and limited resources. Readers learn the patience, dedication, and innovative solutions required to establish successful off-grid gardens, vertical farming systems, and aquaponic setups. These stories humanize growing one's sustenance, emphasizing the joys of harvesting a homegrown meal while acknowledging the practical considerations and hard work involved.

Additionally, real-life experiences shed light on the critical aspect of water management in off-grid living. The narratives detail off-grinders' efforts in designing, implementing, and troubleshooting rainwater harvesting systems. Readers learn from the successes and setbacks, gaining valuable knowledge about the importance of water conservation, purification techniques, and the strategic placement of collection infrastructure. These accounts serve as practical guides for individuals looking to establish their off-grid water solutions, emphasizing the need for careful planning and ongoing maintenance.

Transportation, often a logistical challenge in remote locations, becomes a tangible subject through real-life experiences. The chapter unfolds narratives of individuals constructing and utilizing DIY electric bikes and vehicles, sharing the trials and triumphs of sustainable mobility solutions. Readers witness the evolution of transportation strategies, learning not only about the technical aspects of building eco-friendly modes of travel but also about the lifestyle adjustments and community engagement accompanying such initiatives.

Waste management and composting, central to off-grid sustainability, come to life through the stories of individuals who have successfully implemented zero- waste practices. These narratives detail the creative solutions employed to minimize, reuse, and recycle waste in off-grid settings. Readers gain practical insights into the challenges of responsible waste management, the construction of composting toilets, and integrating recycling practices into daily life. Real-life experiences in waste reduction underscore the importance of mindful consumption and responsible disposal, inspiring readers to adopt similar practices in their off-grid ventures.

Communication and connectivity, often underestimated in off-grid living, become tangible through the recounted experiences of individuals overcoming the limitations of remote locations. These narratives explore off-grinders' ingenuity in establishing reliable communication channels, from satellite technologies to community networks. Readers learn about the practical considerations of staying connected for emergencies and maintaining a sense of community and access to information. Real-life experiences in off-grid communication emphasize the balance between connectivity and the desire for solitude inherent in the off-grid lifestyle.

Beyond individual experiences, the chapter also delves into the communal aspect of off-grid living. Real-life stories highlight the formation and sustenance of off-grid communities, offering a glimpse into the shared values, collaborative efforts, and support networks that characterize these intentional living arrangements. Readers learn about the social dynamics, shared responsibilities, and the collective vision that bind off-grid communities together. These narratives serve as a source of inspiration for individuals contemplating communal living, illustrating the potential for collaborative solutions and a sense of belonging in off-grid communities.

Moreover, the narratives in this section illuminate the financial considerations and budgeting aspects of off-grid living. Real-life experiences delve into the upfront costs, ongoing expenses, and financial strategies individuals and families employ to sustain their off-grid lifestyles. Readers gain practical insights into budgeting for solar installations, sustainable food production, water management systems, and other essential components of off-grid living. These real-life financial narratives provide a grounded perspective on the economic aspects of transitioning to and maintaining an off-grid lifestyle.

"Learning from Real-Life Experiences" encapsulates the essence of the off-grid journey through the lived stories of those who have embraced this lifestyle. The narratives, rich in detail and authenticity, serve as a reservoir of practical knowledge, emotional insights, and inspiration for readers embarking on their off-grid adventures. By connecting with the real-life experiences of off-grinders, readers gain a profound understanding of the challenges and rewards inherent in sustainable, self-sufficient living, empowering them to embark on their off-grid journeys with a wealth of experiential wisdom at their disposal.

Inspiring Others to Embrace Sustainable Living

The chapter on "Inspiring Others to Embrace Sustainable Living" is a powerful testament to the ripple effect that individual choices and lifestyles can have on the broader community. By delving into stories of individuals and communities actively embodying sustainability principles, this section aims to ignite a spark of inspiration in readers, encouraging them to envision and embark on their journeys toward a more sustainable and eco-conscious existence.

Real-life narratives within this chapter unveil the transformative power of leading by example. Individuals who have embraced sustainable living share their stories, detailing the shifts in mindset, lifestyle choices, and daily practices that have led to a more environmentally conscious and harmonious way of life. These stories serve as beacons of hope, illustrating that the path to sustainability is not an unattainable ideal but a series of intentional choices made by ordinary individuals committed to positively impacting the planet.

Moreover, the section explores the role of sustainable housing as a catalyst for inspiration. Real-life experiences showcase individuals designing and building eco-friendly homes, employing energy-efficient technologies, and utilizing recycled materials. These narratives highlight the tangible benefits of sustainable housing in terms of reduced energy consumption and environmental impact and inspire readers to reconsider their living spaces. The stories underscore that sustainable living is not confined to remote off-grid locations; it can be woven into the fabric of urban and suburban life, encouraging a broader shift toward eco-conscious living.

This section's cultivation of sustainable food sources emerges as a compelling narrative. Real-life stories delve into the practices of individuals growing their food, cultivating community gardens, and participating in local agriculture initiatives. These narratives illustrate the empowering journey of reconnecting with the food we consume, promoting food security, and fostering a deeper appreciation for the ecological cycles that sustain us. By showcasing the joys and rewards of sustainable food production, these stories inspire readers to explore their capacity for cultivating a symbiotic relationship with the land and their sustenance.

Transportation, a significant contributor to environmental impact, becomes a focal point for inspiration within the chapter. Real-life accounts feature individuals adopting eco-friendly modes of transportation, from cycling and walking to electric vehicles and car-sharing initiatives. These stories illuminate the myriad ways sustainable transportation choices reduce carbon footprints and contribute to healthier lifestyles and more vibrant communities. By sharing these experiences, the chapter aims to inspire readers to reconsider their commuting habits and explore alternative, earth-friendly transportation options.

Waste reduction and recycling initiatives take center stage in narratives that showcase the transformative power of conscious consumption. Real-life stories detail individuals adopting zero-waste lifestyles, upcycling materials, and participating in community recycling programs. These accounts illustrate that reducing waste is not merely an individual endeavor but a communal effort that can lead to cleaner environments, reduced landfill contributions, and a more sustainable approach to resource use. By sharing these stories, the chapter inspires readers to reassess their consumption patterns and explore creative ways to minimize their ecological footprint.

In addition to individual efforts, the section explores the role of communities in inspiring sustainable living. Real-life narratives highlight the emergence of eco-villages, sustainable neighborhoods, and intentional communities prioritizing environmental stewardship and social cohesion. These stories showcase the collective power of like-minded individuals coming together to create living spaces that reflect shared values of sustainability, resilience, and community engagement. By exploring these narratives, the chapter encourages readers to envision and actively participate in forming such intentional communities, fostering a shared responsibility for sustainable living.

Incorporating sustainable practices in business and entrepreneurship emerges as a source of inspiration within this section. Real-life stories detail the journeys of individuals and organizations adopting eco-friendly business models, promoting sustainable products, and prioritizing environmental and social responsibility. These narratives showcase that sustainability is not confined to personal lifestyles but can permeate professional endeavors, inspiring readers to explore ways to align their work with principles of ecological consciousness and ethical business practices.

Education and community outreach serve as potent tools for inspiring sustainable living. Real-life experiences detail the efforts of individuals actively engaging with their communities to raise awareness about environmental issues, promote sustainable practices, and encourage collective action. These narratives illustrate the transformative impact of education in shaping mindsets and fostering a sense of shared responsibility for the planet. By sharing these stories, the chapter underscores each individual's role in inspiring others to adopt more sustainable lifestyles through education, advocacy, and community building.

Furthermore, the chapter explores the intersection of sustainable living with technology and innovation. Real-life narratives highlight the contributions of individuals and communities leveraging technological advancements to create solutions for environmental challenges. From smart home technologies to eco-friendly apps and platforms, these stories showcase the potential for innovation to complement and enhance sustainable living practices. By sharing these experiences, the chapter aims to inspire readers to explore the intersection of technology and sustainability, fostering a future where advancements contribute positively to ecological balance.

Celebrating cultural diversity within sustainable living serves as a final thread in the tapestry of inspiration. Real-life accounts showcase how various cultures worldwide have integrated sustainable practices into their traditional ways of life. From indigenous communities with deep connections to nature to urban cultures embracing eco-conscious living, these narratives highlight the universality of sustainability principles and the diverse ways in which individuals across the globe are actively contributing to a more harmonious relationship with the planet.

In conclusion, "Inspiring Others to Embrace Sustainable Living" serves as a compendium of stories illuminating the myriad ways individuals and communities actively embrace and promote sustainable living. Through real-life experiences, readers are invited to witness the tangible impacts of intentional choices, demonstrating that sustainable living is not an abstract concept but a lived reality for many. By showcasing these narratives, the chapter seeks to ignite a spark within readers, inspiring them to reimagine their lifestyles, make conscious choices, and actively contribute to the collective effort toward a more sustainable, regenerative, and harmonious world.

CONCLUSION

Within the ever-evolving narrative of sustainable living, "Off-Grid Oasis: DIY Projects for Sustainable Living" develops as a handbook and a manifesto for individuals looking to empower themselves via creative solutions for off-grid independence. The voyage through the many parts of this e-book takes the reader across the worlds of off-grid necessities, renewable energy, sustainable building, and many do-it-yourself projects that reinvent the notion of contemporary life. As we get to the end of this investigation, it becomes clear that the Off-Grid Oasis is more than just a collection of instructions; it is a rallying cry, an invitation to form a new connection with the environment and a road map toward achieving self-sufficiency.

The three defining characteristics of off-grid life are the profound connection to nature, the purposeful acceptance of sustainability, and the steadfast dedication to self-reliance. Every chapter in this electronic book contributes to enabling individuals to take responsibility for their energy, water, housing, and other day-to-day requirements. The entire character of the off-grid lifestyle is reflected in the multidimensional approach, which encompasses solar and wind power, micro-hydro generation, rainwater gathering, well digging, sustainable building, and other methods.

The book "Off-Grid Oasis" is, at its core, a celebration of autonomy. It encourages readers to break free from traditional utility grids' constraints and embrace a life in which resourcefulness, creativity, and environmental stewardship are at the forefront of their lives. The revolutionary potential of renewable energy sources is revealed through the investigation of solar power fundamentals, wind power systems, and micro-hydro generation. These sources are positioned not just as alternatives but also as the foundations of a robust and sustainable future.

Rainwater collection, well digging, gardening, permaculture practices, composting, recycling, and sustainable house construction are some of the themes covered in this e-book, which expands its scope beyond the energy sphere to incorporate other aspects of sustainable living. It is a tribute to the concept that sustainability is not a far-off ideal but rather an actual and attainable reality that each chapter, with its abundance of knowledge and practical ideas, serves as a monument to.

As readers explore the complexities of off-grid agriculture, permaculture practices, and sustainable building, a story of living in peace with the natural world emerges. The principles of permaculture, which focus on ecological design, biodiversity, and activities that promote regenerative growth, serve as a roadmap for creating communities that are not only gardens but also living ecosystems. Similarly, investigating environmentally responsible building practices for residential construction enlightens readers on novel building materials, construction techniques, and architectural designs that harmonize with the natural world.

The electronic book embraces the notion of minimalism and deliberate living. Chapters are devoted to small dwellings, communication solutions, do-it-yourself electronics, and first aid in off-grid scenarios. The belief that "less is more" is embodied by tiny houses, which emphasize simplicity and efficiency. This ideology challenges the rules of society and encourages individuals to emphasize experiences rather than goods. In the digital era, when connectivity and innovation have become tools for empowerment, the chapters on communication solutions and do-it-yourself electronics highlight the significance of self-sufficiency as a critical component of a successful life.

Recognizing that self-sufficiency encompasses one's health and well-being, the section on first aid in off-grid life emphasizes the need to be prepared for unexpected crises. An acknowledgment that genuine independence requires not just living off the grid but also being resilient in the face of unanticipated obstacles is included in the e-book, which offers insights into first aid procedures, evacuation strategies, and survival skills.

It is becoming increasingly clear that the e-book is a complete toolset for persons who desire a life connected with sustainability, innovation, and self-reliance. This realization comes about when we reflect on the journey that went into creating the Off-Grid Oasis. It demonstrates the transforming potential of taking charge of one's energy sources, growing the land, building dwellings that are sympathetic to the environment, and adopting a mentality that places a high value on resourcefulness and resilience.

"Off-Grid Oasis" crafts a story that goes beyond the individual chapters, allowing readers to embark on a journey that is both comprehensive and transformational. This narrative is woven into the vast fabric of sustainable living. The electronic book acts as a guidepost for those looking for not just a change in their way of life but also a paradigm shift in how they interact with the world that surrounds them. It is a reminder that the route to off-grid independence is not merely a technological activity but rather a fundamental reconnection with the Earth and a desire to have a good effect on future generations. This is a reminder that is both important and necessary.

A monument to the strength of individual agency in crafting a sustainable and resilient future, "Off-Grid Oasis: DIY Projects for Sustainable Living" serves as a testament to the power of sustainable living. The reader is inspired to take on the role of creators, inventors, and stewards of the Earth via reading this book. The lifestyle of living off the grid is not only a trend; it is a significant change in consciousness, a proclamation that individuals can build a new narrative—one that emphasizes sustainability, self-sufficiency, and peaceful cohabitation with the natural world. As the last chapters of this electronic book come to a close, the Off-Grid Oasis encourages readers to go on a journey equipped with information, creativity, and a revitalized sense of purpose, prepared to construct their existence that is both sustainable and empowered.